50 Fruit Recipes for Home

By: Kelly Johnson

Table of Contents

- Classic Apple Pie
- Mango Salsa
- Blueberry Pancakes
- Strawberry Spinach Salad
- Banana Bread
- Peach Cobbler
- Watermelon Gazpacho
- Raspberry Lemonade
- Mixed Berry Smoothie Bowl
- Grilled Pineapple Skewers
- Cherry Clafoutis
- Orange Glazed Salmon
- Kiwi Sorbet
- Caramelized Fig and Goat Cheese Pizza
- Cranberry Orange Muffins
- Grape and Walnut Chicken Salad
- Pear and Gorgonzola Flatbread
- Melon Prosciutto Skewers
- Lemon Blueberry Cheesecake Bars
- Pomegranate Glazed Chicken
- Apple Cinnamon Oatmeal
- Mango Coconut Rice
- Papaya Lime Sorbet
- Banana Foster Crepes
- Berry Stuffed French Toast
- Honey Lime Grilled Pineapple
- Blackberry Balsamic Chicken
- Apricot Almond Energy Bites
- Strawberry Shortcake
- Mango Avocado Salsa
- Raspberry Chocolate Chip Muffins
- Citrus Salad with Mint
- Plum Ginger Jam
- Apple Pecan Salad
- Peach Barbecue Chicken
- Mango Coconut Chia Pudding

- Blueberry Balsamic Glazed Salmon
- Pineapple Upside-Down Cake
- Cinnamon Apple Chips
- Lemon Raspberry Thumbprint Cookies
- Gingered Pear Muffins
- Mixed Berry Cobb Salad
- Mango Lime Chicken Tacos
- Orange Cranberry Quinoa Salad
- Strawberry Basil Bruschetta
- Peach Basil Sangria
- Caramel Apple Crisp
- Honeydew Mint Cooler
- Coconut Lime Cupcakes
- Passion Fruit Sorbet

Classic Apple Pie

Ingredients:

For the Pie Crust:

- 2 1/2 cups all-purpose flour
- 1 cup (2 sticks) unsalted butter, chilled and cubed
- 1 teaspoon salt
- 1 tablespoon granulated sugar
- 6-8 tablespoons ice water

For the Apple Filling:

- 6-7 medium-sized apples (a mix of Granny Smith and Honeycrisp works well), peeled, cored, and sliced
- 3/4 cup granulated sugar
- 1/4 cup light brown sugar, packed
- 1 teaspoon ground cinnamon
- 1/4 teaspoon ground nutmeg
- 1/4 teaspoon salt
- 1 tablespoon lemon juice
- 2 tablespoons unsalted butter, cut into small pieces

For Assembly:

- 1 egg (for egg wash)
- 1 tablespoon water (for egg wash)
- Additional sugar for sprinkling on top

Instructions:

1. Prepare the Pie Crust:

- In a food processor, combine the flour, salt, and sugar. Pulse a few times to mix.
- Add the chilled, cubed butter and pulse until the mixture resembles coarse crumbs.
- Gradually add ice water, one tablespoon at a time, and pulse until the dough just comes together.

- Divide the dough in half, shape into two discs, wrap in plastic wrap, and refrigerate for at least 1 hour.

2. Preheat the Oven:

    - Preheat your oven to 375°F (190°C).

3. Make the Apple Filling:

    - In a large bowl, toss the sliced apples with lemon juice to prevent browning.
    - In a separate bowl, mix together granulated sugar, brown sugar, cinnamon, nutmeg, and salt.
    - Sprinkle the sugar mixture over the apples and toss until the apples are evenly coated.

4. Roll Out the Pie Crust:

    - On a floured surface, roll out one disc of the chilled pie dough to fit a 9-inch pie dish. Place the rolled-out dough into the pie dish.

5. Fill the Pie:

    - Spoon the prepared apple filling into the pie crust, mounding it slightly in the center.
    - Dot the top of the apple filling with small pieces of butter.

6. Top with Second Crust:

    - Roll out the second disc of pie dough and place it over the apple filling. Trim the excess dough and crimp the edges to seal the pie.

7. Create Ventilation:

    - Cut slits or create a decorative pattern on the top crust to allow steam to escape during baking.

8. Egg Wash:

    - In a small bowl, whisk together the egg and water to create an egg wash. Brush the top crust with the egg wash.

9. Bake:

- Place the pie on a baking sheet to catch any drips and bake in the preheated oven for 45-50 minutes, or until the crust is golden brown and the filling is bubbly.

10. Cool:

- Allow the pie to cool for at least 3 hours before slicing. This helps the filling set.

11. Serve:

- Serve the classic apple pie on its own or with a scoop of vanilla ice cream for an extra treat.

Enjoy your delicious homemade classic apple pie!

Mango Salsa Recipe

Ingredients:

- 2 ripe mangoes, peeled, pitted, and diced
- 1 red bell pepper, diced
- 1/2 red onion, finely chopped
- 1 jalapeño pepper, seeded and minced
- 1/4 cup fresh cilantro, chopped
- Juice of 2 limes
- Salt and pepper to taste

Instructions:

Prepare the Mango:
- Peel the mangoes and cut the flesh away from the pit. Dice the mango into small, bite-sized pieces.

Chop Vegetables:
- Dice the red bell pepper into small pieces.
- Finely chop the red onion.
- Mince the jalapeño pepper after removing the seeds for milder heat.

Combine Ingredients:
- In a mixing bowl, combine the diced mango, red bell pepper, red onion, jalapeño, and chopped cilantro.

Add Lime Juice:
- Squeeze the juice of two limes over the mixture. Adjust the amount of lime juice based on your preference for acidity.

Season:
- Season the salsa with salt and pepper to taste. Mix well to combine all the flavors.

Chill:
- For optimal flavor, cover the bowl with plastic wrap and let the mango salsa chill in the refrigerator for at least 30 minutes. This allows the flavors to meld together.

Serve:
- Once chilled, give the salsa a final stir and taste for seasoning. Adjust lime, salt, or pepper if needed.
- Serve the mango salsa as a topping for grilled chicken or fish, as a dip with tortilla chips, or as a vibrant side dish.

Optional Additions:

- Feel free to customize your mango salsa by adding ingredients like diced avocado, black beans, or corn for extra texture and flavor.

This mango salsa is not only delicious but also versatile, adding a burst of freshness to various dishes. Enjoy!

Blueberry Pancakes Recipe

Ingredients:

- 1 cup all-purpose flour
- 2 tablespoons granulated sugar
- 1 teaspoon baking powder
- 1/2 teaspoon baking soda
- 1/4 teaspoon salt
- 3/4 cup buttermilk
- 1 large egg
- 2 tablespoons unsalted butter, melted
- 1 teaspoon vanilla extract
- 1 cup fresh blueberries (or thawed frozen blueberries)

Instructions:

Preheat the Griddle or Pan:

- Preheat a griddle or non-stick pan over medium heat.

Prepare Dry Ingredients:

- In a large mixing bowl, whisk together the flour, sugar, baking powder, baking soda, and salt.

Mix Wet Ingredients:

- In a separate bowl, whisk together the buttermilk, egg, melted butter, and vanilla extract until well combined.

Combine Wet and Dry Ingredients:

- Pour the wet ingredients into the dry ingredients and gently stir until just combined. It's okay if there are a few lumps.

Add Blueberries:

- Gently fold in the fresh blueberries. If using frozen blueberries, fold them in gently to avoid discoloring the batter.

Cook Pancakes:

- Lightly grease the griddle or pan with butter or cooking spray.
- Pour 1/4 cup of batter onto the griddle for each pancake. Use the back of a spoon to spread the batter into a round shape.
- Cook until bubbles form on the surface of the pancake, then flip and cook the other side until golden brown.

Keep Warm:

- Transfer the cooked pancakes to a plate and cover with a clean kitchen towel to keep them warm while cooking the remaining batter.

Serve:

- Serve the blueberry pancakes warm with your favorite toppings, such as maple syrup, additional fresh blueberries, or a dollop of whipped cream.

Optional Enhancements:

- Consider adding a sprinkle of cinnamon or lemon zest to the batter for extra flavor.

Enjoy these fluffy and flavorful blueberry pancakes for a delightful breakfast or brunch treat!

Strawberry Spinach Salad Recipe

Ingredients:

For the Salad:

- 6 cups fresh baby spinach, washed and dried
- 2 cups fresh strawberries, hulled and sliced
- 1/2 cup crumbled feta cheese
- 1/2 cup chopped pecans or walnuts, toasted
- 1/4 cup red onion, thinly sliced

For the Dressing:

- 1/4 cup extra-virgin olive oil
- 2 tablespoons balsamic vinegar
- 1 tablespoon honey
- 1 teaspoon Dijon mustard
- Salt and black pepper to taste

Instructions:

1. Prepare the Salad Ingredients:

- Wash and dry the baby spinach. Hull and slice the fresh strawberries. Crumble the feta cheese, chop the nuts, and thinly slice the red onion.

2. Toast the Nuts:

- In a dry skillet over medium heat, toast the chopped nuts until fragrant and lightly browned. Stir frequently to prevent burning. Remove from heat and let them cool.

3. Assemble the Salad:

- In a large salad bowl, combine the baby spinach, sliced strawberries, crumbled feta cheese, toasted nuts, and sliced red onion.

4. Prepare the Dressing:

- In a small bowl, whisk together the extra-virgin olive oil, balsamic vinegar, honey, Dijon mustard, salt, and black pepper. Adjust the seasoning to taste.

5. Dress the Salad:

- Drizzle the dressing over the salad ingredients. Toss gently to coat the salad evenly with the dressing.

6. Serve:

- Transfer the strawberry spinach salad to individual serving plates or a large serving platter.

7. Optional Additions:

- Consider adding grilled chicken or shrimp for a protein boost.
- Add avocado slices for extra creaminess.

8. Enjoy:

- Serve the strawberry spinach salad immediately, and enjoy the refreshing combination of sweet strawberries, crisp spinach, and the savory elements of feta and nuts.

This salad is perfect for a light lunch or as a side dish for a summer meal. It brings together the sweetness of strawberries with the earthiness of spinach for a delightful and healthy combination.

Classic Banana Bread Recipe

Ingredients:

- 3 ripe bananas, mashed
- 1/2 cup unsalted butter, melted
- 1 teaspoon vanilla extract
- 1 cup granulated sugar
- 1 large egg, beaten
- 1 1/2 cups all-purpose flour
- 1 teaspoon baking soda
- 1/4 teaspoon salt
- Optional: 1/2 cup chopped nuts (walnuts or pecans)

Instructions:

1. Preheat the Oven:

- Preheat your oven to 350°F (175°C). Grease a 9x5-inch (23x13 cm) loaf pan.

2. Mash the Bananas:

- In a large mixing bowl, mash the ripe bananas with a fork or potato masher until smooth.

3. Add Wet Ingredients:

- Add the melted butter to the mashed bananas and mix well.
- Stir in the beaten egg and vanilla extract until the mixture is well combined.

4. Combine Dry Ingredients:

- In a separate bowl, whisk together the flour, baking soda, and salt.

5. Mix Batter:

    - Add the dry ingredients to the banana mixture and stir until just combined. Be careful not to overmix; a few lumps are okay.
    - If using nuts, fold them into the batter.

6. Pour into the Pan:

    - Pour the batter into the greased loaf pan, spreading it evenly.

7. Bake:

    - Bake in the preheated oven for approximately 60-65 minutes or until a toothpick inserted into the center comes out clean or with a few moist crumbs.

8. Cool:

    - Allow the banana bread to cool in the pan for about 10 minutes before transferring it to a wire rack to cool completely.

9. Slice and Serve:

    - Once completely cooled, slice the banana bread into even slices and serve.

10. Optional: Additions and Variations:

    - For added flavor, consider adding chocolate chips or dried fruit to the batter.
    - Sprinkle a handful of chopped nuts on top before baking for a crunchy crust.

11. Storage:

- Store leftover banana bread in an airtight container at room temperature for a few days. You can also refrigerate or freeze for longer storage.

Enjoy your homemade classic banana bread with a cup of coffee or tea!

Classic Peach Cobbler Recipe

Ingredients:

For the Peach Filling:

- 6-8 fresh peaches, peeled, pitted, and sliced (or 1.5 pounds frozen peach slices, thawed)
- 1/2 cup granulated sugar
- 1 tablespoon lemon juice
- 1 teaspoon vanilla extract
- 1/4 teaspoon ground cinnamon
- 2 tablespoons all-purpose flour (to thicken, adjust as needed)

For the Cobbler Topping:

- 1 cup all-purpose flour
- 1/2 cup granulated sugar
- 1 teaspoon baking powder
- 1/4 teaspoon salt
- 1/2 cup unsalted butter, melted
- 1/4 cup boiling water

Optional Topping:

- Vanilla ice cream or whipped cream for serving

Instructions:

1. Preheat the Oven:

- Preheat your oven to 375°F (190°C).

2. Prepare the Peach Filling:

    - In a large mixing bowl, combine the sliced peaches, granulated sugar, lemon juice, vanilla extract, ground cinnamon, and flour. Toss until the peaches are well coated. Set aside and let them sit for a few minutes.

3. Transfer to Baking Dish:

    - Pour the peach mixture into a greased 9x13-inch (23x33 cm) baking dish or a similar-sized casserole dish, spreading it evenly.

4. Make the Cobbler Topping:

    - In a separate bowl, whisk together the flour, sugar, baking powder, and salt for the cobbler topping.
    - Add the melted butter to the dry ingredients and stir until combined.
    - Pour in the boiling water and mix until smooth.

5. Spoon over Peaches:

    - Spoon the cobbler topping evenly over the peach mixture. It's okay if it doesn't cover the peaches completely; it will spread during baking.

6. Bake:

    - Bake in the preheated oven for 40-45 minutes or until the topping is golden brown and the peach filling is bubbling.

7. Cool Slightly:

- Allow the peach cobbler to cool for 10-15 minutes before serving. This helps the filling set.

8. Serve:

- Serve warm, either on its own or with a scoop of vanilla ice cream or a dollop of whipped cream.

9. Enjoy:

- Enjoy the classic peach cobbler as a delightful dessert, perfect for any occasion.

This peach cobbler recipe captures the essence of sweet, juicy peaches with a golden, buttery topping, creating a comforting and delicious treat.

Watermelon Gazpacho Recipe

Ingredients:

For the Gazpacho:

- 4 cups seedless watermelon, diced
- 1 cucumber, peeled, seeded, and diced
- 1 red bell pepper, diced
- 1 small red onion, finely chopped
- 2 tomatoes, diced
- 2 cloves garlic, minced
- 1/4 cup fresh cilantro, chopped
- 1/4 cup fresh mint, chopped
- 3 cups tomato juice
- 1/4 cup red wine vinegar
- 1/4 cup extra-virgin olive oil
- Salt and pepper to taste
- Dash of hot sauce (optional, for extra heat)

For Garnish:

- Crumbled feta cheese
- Additional diced cucumber
- Fresh mint leaves

Instructions:

1. Prepare the Ingredients:

- Dice the watermelon, cucumber, red bell pepper, tomatoes, and onion according to the specifications listed.

2. Blend Watermelon Base:

- In a blender or food processor, puree 2 cups of diced watermelon until smooth. Transfer to a large mixing bowl.

3. Add Vegetables and Herbs:

- Add the remaining diced watermelon, cucumber, red bell pepper, tomatoes, minced garlic, chopped cilantro, and chopped mint to the bowl.

4. Mix Tomato Juice, Vinegar, and Olive Oil:

- In a separate bowl, combine tomato juice, red wine vinegar, and extra-virgin olive oil. Whisk together until well combined.

5. Combine and Season:

- Pour the tomato juice mixture over the watermelon and vegetable mixture. Stir well to combine.
- Season the gazpacho with salt and pepper to taste. Add a dash of hot sauce if you desire extra heat.

6. Chill:

- Cover the bowl and refrigerate the gazpacho for at least 2 hours, allowing the flavors to meld and the soup to chill.

7. Serve:

- Stir the gazpacho before serving. Ladle the chilled soup into bowls.

8. Garnish:

- Garnish each serving with crumbled feta cheese, additional diced cucumber, and fresh mint leaves.

9. Enjoy:

- Serve the refreshing watermelon gazpacho as a light and flavorful appetizer or a cooling soup on a warm day.

This watermelon gazpacho is a delightful twist on the classic Spanish cold soup, incorporating the sweet and juicy flavors of watermelon for a refreshing and summery dish.

Raspberry Lemonade Recipe

Ingredients:

For the Raspberry Syrup:

- 1 cup fresh raspberries
- 1/2 cup granulated sugar
- 1/2 cup water

For the Lemonade:

- 1 cup freshly squeezed lemon juice (about 4-6 lemons)
- 1 cup granulated sugar (adjust to taste)
- 6 cups cold water
- Ice cubes
- Fresh raspberries and lemon slices for garnish

Instructions:

1. Make Raspberry Syrup:

- In a small saucepan, combine the fresh raspberries, sugar, and water.
- Bring the mixture to a gentle boil over medium heat, stirring occasionally.
- Reduce heat and let it simmer for 5-7 minutes until the raspberries break down and the sugar dissolves.
- Strain the syrup through a fine mesh sieve into a bowl, pressing on the solids to extract as much liquid as possible. Discard the remaining solids.

2. Prepare Lemonade:

- In a large pitcher, combine the freshly squeezed lemon juice and granulated sugar. Stir until the sugar dissolves.

3. Mix Raspberry Lemonade:

- Pour the raspberry syrup into the lemon mixture and stir well to combine.
- Add cold water to the pitcher and mix until everything is well incorporated.

4. Adjust Sweetness:

- Taste the raspberry lemonade and adjust the sweetness by adding more sugar if needed. Stir until fully dissolved.

5. Chill:

- Refrigerate the raspberry lemonade for at least 1-2 hours to allow the flavors to meld and the drink to chill.

6. Serve:

- Fill glasses with ice cubes and pour the chilled raspberry lemonade over the ice.

7. Garnish:

- Garnish each glass with fresh raspberries and lemon slices.

8. Enjoy:

- Stir the raspberry lemonade before sipping, and enjoy this sweet, tart, and refreshing drink!

Optional Enhancements:

- Add a sprig of fresh mint for an extra burst of flavor.
- If you like a fizzy lemonade, top off each glass with a splash of sparkling water.

This homemade raspberry lemonade is a vibrant and flavorful beverage that's perfect for warm days or as a delightful accompaniment to picnics and gatherings.

Mixed Berry Smoothie Bowl Recipe

Ingredients:

For the Smoothie Base:

- 1 cup frozen mixed berries (strawberries, blueberries, raspberries, and blackberries)
- 1 ripe banana, frozen
- 1/2 cup Greek yogurt
- 1/2 cup almond milk (or any milk of your choice)
- 1 tablespoon honey or maple syrup (optional, for added sweetness)
- 1 teaspoon chia seeds (optional, for texture)

For Toppings:

- Fresh berries (blueberries, raspberries, sliced strawberries, etc.)
- Granola
- Sliced banana
- Coconut flakes
- Chopped nuts (almonds, walnuts, or your choice)
- Drizzle of honey or nut butter

Instructions:

1. Prepare the Smoothie Base:

- In a blender, combine the frozen mixed berries, frozen banana, Greek yogurt, almond milk, and optional honey or maple syrup.
- Blend until smooth and creamy. If the mixture is too thick, you can add more almond milk a little at a time until you reach your desired consistency.
- Optionally, stir in chia seeds for added texture and nutritional benefits.

2. Pour into a Bowl:

- Pour the smoothie base into a bowl.

3. Add Toppings:

- Arrange a variety of toppings on the smoothie base. Get creative and use a mix of fresh berries, granola, sliced banana, coconut flakes, chopped nuts, and any other toppings you enjoy.

4. Drizzle with Honey or Nut Butter:

- Drizzle a bit of honey or your favorite nut butter over the top for extra sweetness and flavor.

5. Serve Immediately:

- Enjoy your mixed berry smoothie bowl immediately with a spoon!

Optional Enhancements:

- Add a handful of spinach or kale to the smoothie base for an extra nutrient boost without affecting the flavor.
- Include a scoop of protein powder if you want to increase the protein content of your smoothie bowl.

This mixed berry smoothie bowl is not only delicious but also customizable to your taste preferences. It's a nutritious and vibrant breakfast or snack option that's both satisfying and visually appealing.

Grilled Pineapple Skewers Recipe

Ingredients:

- 1 large pineapple, peeled, cored, and cut into bite-sized chunks
- 1/4 cup honey or maple syrup
- 2 tablespoons melted butter or coconut oil
- 1 teaspoon ground cinnamon
- Wooden or metal skewers

Instructions:

1. Preheat the Grill:

- Preheat your grill to medium-high heat.

2. Prepare the Pineapple:

- Cut the pineapple into bite-sized chunks, ensuring the core is removed.

3. Make the Marinade:

- In a small bowl, whisk together the honey or maple syrup, melted butter or coconut oil, and ground cinnamon to create the marinade.

4. Skewer the Pineapple:

- Thread the pineapple chunks onto skewers, leaving some space between each piece.

5. Brush with Marinade:

- Place the pineapple skewers on a tray and brush them generously with the prepared marinade. Ensure each piece is coated evenly.

6. Grill the Pineapple:

- Place the skewers on the preheated grill. Grill for about 2-3 minutes on each side or until you see grill marks and the pineapple caramelizes slightly.

7. Baste with Marinade:

- During grilling, continue to baste the pineapple skewers with the remaining marinade to enhance flavor.

8. Remove from Grill:

- Once the pineapple is grilled to your liking, remove the skewers from the grill and place them on a serving platter.

9. Serve Warm:

- Serve the grilled pineapple skewers warm. They can be enjoyed on their own or paired with a scoop of vanilla ice cream for a delightful dessert.

10. Optional Garnish:

- Garnish with a sprinkle of cinnamon or a drizzle of extra honey before serving.

11. Enjoy:

- Enjoy the deliciously caramelized and smoky flavor of your grilled pineapple skewers!

Grilled pineapple skewers make for a sweet and tropical treat, perfect for outdoor gatherings, BBQs, or a simple and flavorful dessert.

Cherry Clafoutis Recipe

Ingredients:

- 2 cups fresh or frozen cherries, pitted
- 3 large eggs
- 1 cup whole milk
- 1/2 cup granulated sugar
- 1 teaspoon vanilla extract
- 1/2 cup all-purpose flour
- Pinch of salt
- Butter for greasing the baking dish
- Powdered sugar for dusting (optional)

Instructions:

1. Preheat the Oven:

- Preheat your oven to 350°F (175°C). Butter a baking dish (typically a 9-inch round dish).

2. Prepare the Cherries:

- If using fresh cherries, wash and pit them. If using frozen cherries, make sure they are thawed and drained.

3. Arrange Cherries in Baking Dish:

- Spread the pitted cherries evenly in the buttered baking dish.

4. Make the Batter:

- In a blender or mixing bowl, combine the eggs, whole milk, granulated sugar, vanilla extract, flour, and a pinch of salt.
- Blend or whisk until you have a smooth batter with no lumps.

5. Pour Batter Over Cherries:

- Pour the batter over the arranged cherries in the baking dish. The cherries will naturally sink to the bottom as the clafoutis bakes.

6. Bake:

- Place the baking dish in the preheated oven and bake for about 40-45 minutes or until the clafoutis is puffed, set in the center, and has a golden-brown color.

7. Cool Slightly:

- Remove the clafoutis from the oven and let it cool slightly. It will sink as it cools.

8. Dust with Powdered Sugar (Optional):

- Dust the top of the clafoutis with powdered sugar for a decorative touch. This step is optional.

9. Serve Warm:

- Serve the cherry clafoutis warm. It can be enjoyed on its own or with a dollop of whipped cream or a scoop of vanilla ice cream.

10. Enjoy:

- Enjoy the classic French dessert with the rich, custard-like texture and the sweet burst of cherries.

Cherry clafoutis is a simple and elegant dessert that celebrates the deliciousness of ripe cherries. It's a delightful treat to share with family and friends.

Orange Glazed Salmon Recipe

Ingredients:

For the Salmon:

- 4 salmon fillets, skin-on or skinless
- Salt and black pepper to taste
- 2 tablespoons olive oil

For the Orange Glaze:

- 1/2 cup freshly squeezed orange juice (about 2 large oranges)
- Zest of one orange
- 2 tablespoons soy sauce
- 2 tablespoons honey
- 1 tablespoon Dijon mustard
- 2 cloves garlic, minced
- 1 teaspoon grated fresh ginger
- 1 tablespoon olive oil (for cooking the glaze)

For Garnish:

- Fresh chopped parsley or green onions (optional)

Instructions:

1. Preheat the Oven:

- Preheat your oven to 400°F (200°C).

2. Season the Salmon:

- Pat the salmon fillets dry with paper towels. Season both sides with salt and black pepper.

3. Sear Salmon:

- Heat 2 tablespoons of olive oil in an oven-safe skillet over medium-high heat. Once hot, add the salmon fillets, skin-side down if applicable, and sear for 2-3 minutes until the edges start to brown.

4. Make the Orange Glaze:

- In a small bowl, whisk together the orange juice, orange zest, soy sauce, honey, Dijon mustard, minced garlic, and grated ginger.

5. Glaze the Salmon:

- Pour half of the orange glaze over the salmon fillets. Reserve the remaining glaze for later.

6. Transfer to Oven:

- Transfer the skillet to the preheated oven and bake for 10-12 minutes, or until the salmon is cooked through and flakes easily with a fork.

7. Glaze Again:

- In the last 5 minutes of baking, brush the salmon with the remaining orange glaze.

8. Garnish and Serve:

- Once the salmon is done, remove it from the oven. Garnish with fresh chopped parsley or green onions if desired.

9. Serve Warm:

- Serve the orange glazed salmon warm over a bed of rice or with your favorite side dishes.

10. Enjoy:

- Enjoy this flavorful and citrusy glazed salmon that perfectly balances sweet, tangy, and savory notes.

This orange glazed salmon is a delightful dish that brings a burst of citrusy freshness to your dinner table. It's quick to make and perfect for both weeknight dinners and special occasions.

Kiwi Sorbet Recipe

Ingredients:

- 6 ripe kiwis, peeled and sliced
- 1/2 cup granulated sugar (adjust to taste)
- 1/2 cup water
- 1 tablespoon fresh lime or lemon juice

Instructions:

1. Prepare the Kiwis:

- Peel the kiwis and cut them into slices.

2. Make Simple Syrup:

- In a small saucepan, combine the granulated sugar and water. Heat over medium heat, stirring occasionally, until the sugar completely dissolves. Remove from heat and let the simple syrup cool.

3. Blend Kiwis:

- Place the kiwi slices in a blender or food processor. Blend until you have a smooth puree.

4. Combine Kiwi Puree and Simple Syrup:

- In a mixing bowl, combine the kiwi puree with the cooled simple syrup. Mix well.

5. Add Citrus Juice:

- Stir in the fresh lime or lemon juice. This adds a bright citrus flavor and helps enhance the sweetness.

6. Chill the Mixture:

- Place the mixture in the refrigerator to chill for at least 1-2 hours. This allows the flavors to meld and the mixture to cool.

7. Freeze:

- Pour the chilled kiwi mixture into an ice cream maker and churn according to the manufacturer's instructions until it reaches a sorbet consistency.

8. Transfer to Freezer-Safe Container:

- Transfer the churned kiwi sorbet to a freezer-safe container. Smooth the top with a spatula.

9. Freeze Until Firm:

- Freeze the sorbet for an additional 4-6 hours or overnight until it becomes firm.

10. Serve:

- Scoop the kiwi sorbet into bowls or cones.

11. Garnish (Optional):

- Garnish with fresh kiwi slices or a mint sprig if desired.

12. Enjoy:

- Enjoy the refreshing and tangy flavor of homemade kiwi sorbet!

This kiwi sorbet is a delightful and healthy frozen treat that captures the natural sweetness of ripe kiwis. It's perfect for a hot summer day or as a light and refreshing dessert.

Caramelized Fig and Goat Cheese Pizza

Ingredients:

For the Pizza Dough:

- 1 pound pizza dough (store-bought or homemade)

For the Caramelized Figs:

- 8-10 fresh figs, sliced
- 2 tablespoons unsalted butter
- 2 tablespoons honey
- 1 tablespoon balsamic vinegar
- Pinch of salt

For the Pizza Toppings:

- 1 cup goat cheese, crumbled
- 1/4 cup chopped walnuts or pecans
- Fresh arugula or baby spinach for garnish
- Balsamic glaze for drizzling (optional)

Instructions:

1. Preheat the Oven:

- Preheat your oven to the temperature recommended for your pizza dough (usually around 450°F or 232°C).

2. Caramelize the Figs:

- In a skillet over medium heat, melt the butter. Add the sliced figs, honey, balsamic vinegar, and a pinch of salt.
- Cook the figs for 5-7 minutes, stirring occasionally, until they become caramelized and softened. Remove from heat.

3. Roll Out Pizza Dough:

- Roll out the pizza dough on a floured surface to your desired thickness.

4. Assemble the Pizza:

- Transfer the rolled-out dough to a pizza stone or baking sheet.
- Spread the caramelized figs evenly over the pizza dough.
- Sprinkle crumbled goat cheese and chopped nuts over the figs.

5. Bake:

- Bake in the preheated oven according to your pizza dough instructions or until the crust is golden and the cheese is melted and slightly browned.

6. Garnish:

- Once out of the oven, scatter fresh arugula or baby spinach over the hot pizza.

7. Drizzle with Balsamic Glaze (Optional):

- For an extra layer of flavor, drizzle balsamic glaze over the pizza. This step is optional but highly recommended.

8. Slice and Serve:

- Slice the caramelized fig and goat cheese pizza into wedges and serve immediately.

9. Enjoy:

- Enjoy the unique combination of sweet caramelized figs, tangy goat cheese, and crunchy nuts in this delicious pizza!

This pizza makes for a sophisticated and flavorful dish that's perfect for entertaining or as a special treat. The combination of sweet and savory flavors is sure to delight your taste buds.

Cranberry Orange Muffins Recipe

Ingredients:

Dry Ingredients:

- 2 cups all-purpose flour
- 1 cup granulated sugar
- 1 1/2 teaspoons baking powder
- 1/2 teaspoon baking soda
- 1/4 teaspoon salt

Wet Ingredients:

- 1/2 cup unsalted butter, melted and cooled
- 2 large eggs
- 1 cup plain yogurt (or Greek yogurt)
- Zest of 1 orange
- 1/4 cup fresh orange juice
- 1 teaspoon vanilla extract

Add-Ins:

- 1 1/2 cups fresh or frozen cranberries, coarsely chopped

Optional Topping:

- Additional orange zest
- Coarse sugar for sprinkling

Instructions:

1. Preheat the Oven:

- Preheat your oven to 375°F (190°C). Line a muffin tin with paper liners or grease the muffin cups.

2. Mix Dry Ingredients:

- In a large mixing bowl, whisk together the flour, sugar, baking powder, baking soda, and salt.

3. Combine Wet Ingredients:

    - In another bowl, whisk together the melted butter, eggs, yogurt, orange zest, orange juice, and vanilla extract until well combined.

4. Combine Wet and Dry Ingredients:

    - Pour the wet ingredients into the dry ingredients and gently fold until just combined. Do not overmix.

5. Add Cranberries:

    - Gently fold in the chopped cranberries until evenly distributed in the batter.

6. Fill Muffin Cups:

    - Divide the batter equally among the muffin cups, filling each about two-thirds full.

7. Optional Topping:

    - If desired, sprinkle a little coarse sugar and additional orange zest on top of each muffin for a crunchy and citrusy topping.

8. Bake:

    - Bake in the preheated oven for 18-20 minutes or until a toothpick inserted into the center comes out clean or with a few moist crumbs.

9. Cool:

    - Allow the muffins to cool in the tin for a few minutes before transferring them to a wire rack to cool completely.

10. Enjoy:

- Once cooled, enjoy these moist and flavorful cranberry orange muffins with a cup of tea or coffee.

These muffins are perfect for breakfast, brunch, or as a delightful snack. The combination of tart cranberries and citrusy orange creates a burst of flavor in every bite.

Grape and Walnut Chicken Salad Recipe

Ingredients:

For the Chicken Salad:

- 2 cups cooked chicken breast, shredded or diced
- 1 cup red seedless grapes, halved
- 1/2 cup celery, finely chopped
- 1/2 cup red onion, finely diced
- 1/2 cup walnuts, chopped
- Salt and black pepper to taste

For the Dressing:

- 1/2 cup mayonnaise
- 2 tablespoons Greek yogurt (optional for added creaminess)
- 2 tablespoons honey
- 1 tablespoon Dijon mustard
- 1 tablespoon white wine vinegar
- 1/2 teaspoon garlic powder
- Salt and black pepper to taste

For Serving:

- Fresh lettuce leaves or sandwich bread

Instructions:

1. Prepare the Chicken:

- Cook the chicken breasts (grill, bake, or boil) until fully cooked. Shred or dice the chicken into bite-sized pieces.

2. Make the Dressing:

- In a small bowl, whisk together the mayonnaise, Greek yogurt (if using), honey, Dijon mustard, white wine vinegar, garlic powder, salt, and black pepper. Adjust the sweetness and seasoning according to your taste.

3. Assemble the Salad:

- In a large mixing bowl, combine the cooked chicken, halved grapes, chopped celery, diced red onion, and chopped walnuts.

4. Add Dressing:

- Pour the dressing over the chicken and grape mixture. Gently toss everything together until the ingredients are evenly coated with the dressing.

5. Season:

- Season the chicken salad with additional salt and black pepper to taste.

6. Chill:

- Cover the bowl and refrigerate the chicken salad for at least 1-2 hours to allow the flavors to meld.

7. Serve:

- Serve the grape and walnut chicken salad on a bed of fresh lettuce leaves, in a sandwich, or with crackers.

8. Enjoy:

- Enjoy this refreshing and flavorful chicken salad as a light meal or snack.

Optional Additions:

- Add a handful of fresh herbs like chopped parsley or dill for additional freshness.
- Include a squeeze of fresh lemon juice for a citrusy kick.

This Grape and Walnut Chicken Salad is a perfect combination of sweet and savory flavors, making it a delicious and satisfying dish for any occasion. Serve it in a lettuce cup, sandwich, or enjoy it as a stand-alone salad.

Pear and Gorgonzola Flatbread Recipe

Ingredients:

For the Flatbread:

- 1 pre-made flatbread or pizza crust

For the Toppings:

- 1 large ripe pear, thinly sliced
- 1/2 cup crumbled Gorgonzola cheese
- 1/4 cup chopped walnuts
- 1 tablespoon honey
- Fresh thyme leaves (optional, for garnish)

For the Balsamic Glaze:

- 1/4 cup balsamic vinegar
- 1 tablespoon honey

Instructions:

1. Preheat the Oven:

- Preheat your oven to the temperature recommended for your flatbread or pizza crust (usually around 425°F or 220°C).

2. Prepare the Balsamic Glaze:

- In a small saucepan, combine the balsamic vinegar and honey. Bring to a simmer over medium heat, stirring constantly. Reduce heat to low and let it simmer for 5-7 minutes or until it thickens into a glaze. Remove from heat and set aside.

3. Assemble the Flatbread:

- Place the pre-made flatbread or pizza crust on a baking sheet.

4. Arrange Pear Slices:

- Arrange the thinly sliced pear over the flatbread, ensuring an even distribution.

5. Add Gorgonzola and Walnuts:

    - Sprinkle the crumbled Gorgonzola cheese and chopped walnuts over the pear slices.

6. Bake:

    - Bake in the preheated oven according to the flatbread or pizza crust instructions or until the edges are golden and the cheese has melted.

7. Drizzle with Balsamic Glaze:

    - Once out of the oven, drizzle the balsamic glaze over the pear and Gorgonzola flatbread.

8. Finish with Honey and Thyme:

    - Drizzle honey over the flatbread for added sweetness. Optionally, sprinkle fresh thyme leaves as a garnish.

9. Slice and Serve:

    - Slice the flatbread into wedges and serve immediately.

10. Enjoy:

    - Enjoy this delightful combination of sweet pear, tangy Gorgonzola, and crunchy walnuts in every bite!

This Pear and Gorgonzola Flatbread makes for a sophisticated appetizer or light meal. The combination of flavors is both sweet and savory, creating a delicious balance on your palate.

Melon Prosciutto Skewers

Ingredients:

- 1 cantaloupe or honeydew melon, cut into bite-sized cubes
- 8-10 slices of prosciutto, cut into strips
- Fresh mint leaves, for garnish
- Balsamic glaze, for drizzling (optional)

Instructions:

1. Prepare the Melon:

- Cut the cantaloupe or honeydew melon into bite-sized cubes. Ensure the melon cubes are similar in size for even skewering.

2. Assemble the Skewers:

- Take a cube of melon and wrap a strip of prosciutto around it. Skewer the prosciutto-wrapped melon onto small cocktail sticks or toothpicks.

3. Arrange on a Platter:

- Place the melon and prosciutto skewers on a serving platter.

4. Garnish:

- Garnish the skewers with fresh mint leaves. The mint adds a refreshing element that complements the sweetness of the melon and the savory prosciutto.

5. Drizzle with Balsamic Glaze (Optional):

- If desired, drizzle a small amount of balsamic glaze over the skewers for an extra burst of flavor. The balsamic glaze adds a touch of sweetness and acidity.

6. Serve:

- Arrange the skewers beautifully and serve immediately.

7. Enjoy:

- Enjoy these Melon Prosciutto Skewers as a refreshing and elegant appetizer at your next gathering.

Note:

- You can customize the presentation by arranging the skewers on a bed of arugula or a decorative platter.
- These skewers are a perfect combination of sweet and salty flavors, making them a delightful addition to any party or as a light summer snack.

Lemon Blueberry Cheesecake Bars Recipe

Ingredients:

For the Crust:

- 1 1/2 cups graham cracker crumbs
- 1/3 cup unsalted butter, melted
- 2 tablespoons granulated sugar

For the Cheesecake Filling:

- 16 ounces (2 blocks) cream cheese, softened
- 1 cup granulated sugar
- 2 large eggs
- 1 teaspoon vanilla extract
- Zest of 1 lemon
- 2 tablespoons fresh lemon juice

For the Blueberry Swirl:

- 1 cup fresh or frozen blueberries
- 2 tablespoons granulated sugar
- 1 tablespoon water
- 1 tablespoon lemon juice

Instructions:

1. Preheat the Oven:

- Preheat your oven to 325°F (163°C). Line a 9x9-inch (23x23 cm) baking pan with parchment paper, leaving some overhang for easy removal.

2. Make the Crust:

- In a bowl, combine the graham cracker crumbs, melted butter, and sugar. Press the mixture evenly into the bottom of the prepared pan to form the crust.

3. Bake the Crust:

- Bake the crust in the preheated oven for 10 minutes. Remove from the oven and let it cool while you prepare the filling.

4. Make the Blueberry Swirl:

- In a small saucepan, combine the blueberries, sugar, water, and lemon juice. Cook over medium heat, stirring occasionally, until the blueberries burst and the mixture thickens slightly. Remove from heat and set aside to cool.

5. Prepare the Cheesecake Filling:

- In a large bowl, beat the softened cream cheese until smooth. Add the sugar, eggs, vanilla extract, lemon zest, and lemon juice. Beat until well combined and creamy.

6. Assemble the Bars:

- Pour the cream cheese mixture over the cooled crust. Drop spoonfuls of the blueberry swirl mixture on top. Use a knife or skewer to create a marbled effect by gently swirling the blueberry mixture into the cream cheese.

7. Bake the Cheesecake Bars:

- Bake in the preheated oven for 30-35 minutes or until the center is set. The edges should be slightly golden.

8. Cool and Chill:

- Allow the cheesecake bars to cool in the pan, then refrigerate for at least 4 hours or overnight to set.

9. Slice and Serve:

- Once chilled, lift the cheesecake out of the pan using the parchment paper overhang. Slice into bars.

10. Garnish (Optional):

- Garnish with additional blueberries, lemon zest, or a dusting of powdered sugar if desired.

11. Enjoy:

- Serve these delightful Lemon Blueberry Cheesecake Bars as a refreshing and indulgent treat.

These bars are a perfect combination of creamy cheesecake, zesty lemon, and sweet blueberry swirls, making them a delightful dessert for any occasion.

Pomegranate Glazed Chicken Recipe

Ingredients:

For the Chicken:

- 4 boneless, skinless chicken breasts
- Salt and black pepper to taste
- 2 tablespoons olive oil

For the Pomegranate Glaze:

- 1 cup pomegranate juice
- 1/4 cup honey
- 2 tablespoons soy sauce
- 1 tablespoon Dijon mustard
- 2 cloves garlic, minced
- 1 teaspoon grated fresh ginger
- 1 tablespoon cornstarch (optional, for thickening)

For Garnish:

- Fresh pomegranate arils
- Chopped fresh parsley or cilantro

Instructions:

1. Preheat the Oven:

- Preheat your oven to 375°F (190°C).

2. Season the Chicken:

- Season the chicken breasts with salt and black pepper on both sides.

3. Sear the Chicken:

- In an oven-safe skillet, heat olive oil over medium-high heat. Sear the chicken breasts for 2-3 minutes on each side or until golden brown.

4. Make the Pomegranate Glaze:

   - In a bowl, whisk together pomegranate juice, honey, soy sauce, Dijon mustard, minced garlic, and grated ginger.

5. Glaze the Chicken:

   - Pour half of the pomegranate glaze over the seared chicken in the skillet.

6. Bake:

   - Transfer the skillet to the preheated oven and bake for 15-20 minutes or until the chicken is cooked through.

7. Baste with Glaze:

   - Baste the chicken with the remaining pomegranate glaze during the last 5 minutes of baking for a shiny finish.

8. Optional Thickening:

   - If you prefer a thicker glaze, mix cornstarch with a little water to create a slurry. Add it to the remaining glaze in the skillet and cook on the stovetop until it thickens.

9. Garnish:

   - Once out of the oven, garnish the glazed chicken with fresh pomegranate arils and chopped parsley or cilantro.

10. Serve:

    - Serve the pomegranate glazed chicken over rice, quinoa, or your favorite side dish.

11. Enjoy:

    - Enjoy the sweet and tangy flavor of this Pomegranate Glazed Chicken, a perfect combination of savory and fruity notes!

This dish is not only delicious but also visually stunning, making it a great choice for special occasions or a flavorful weeknight dinner.

Apple Cinnamon Oatmeal Recipe

Ingredients:

- 1 cup old-fashioned rolled oats
- 2 cups milk (dairy or plant-based)
- 1 large apple, peeled, cored, and diced
- 2 tablespoons maple syrup or honey
- 1 teaspoon ground cinnamon
- 1/4 teaspoon ground nutmeg
- Pinch of salt
- Optional toppings: sliced almonds, chopped walnuts, raisins, sliced bananas, or additional diced apples

Instructions:

1. Cook the Oats:

   - In a saucepan, combine the rolled oats and milk. Bring to a gentle boil over medium heat, stirring occasionally.

2. Add Apples:

   - Once the oats begin to simmer, add the diced apple, maple syrup or honey, ground cinnamon, ground nutmeg, and a pinch of salt.

3. Simmer:

   - Reduce the heat to low and let the mixture simmer for about 5-7 minutes, or until the oats are cooked to your desired consistency. Stir occasionally to prevent sticking.

4. Adjust Sweetness:

   - Taste the oatmeal and adjust the sweetness by adding more maple syrup or honey if needed. Stir to combine.

5. Serve:

   - Once the oatmeal is cooked to your liking, remove the saucepan from the heat.

6. Optional Toppings:

- Serve the apple cinnamon oatmeal hot, and top with sliced almonds, chopped walnuts, raisins, sliced bananas, or additional diced apples for extra texture and flavor.

7. Enjoy:

- Enjoy a warm and comforting bowl of homemade apple cinnamon oatmeal, perfect for a wholesome breakfast or a cozy snack.

Note:

- You can customize the oatmeal by adjusting the consistency with more or less milk according to your preference.
- Experiment with different toppings to add variety and nutrition to your oatmeal.

Mango Coconut Rice Recipe

Ingredients:

- 1 cup basmati or jasmine rice
- 1 cup coconut milk
- 1 cup water
- 1 ripe mango, peeled, pitted, and diced
- 2 tablespoons shredded coconut (optional)
- 2 tablespoons sugar (adjust to taste)
- 1/4 teaspoon salt
- Fresh cilantro or mint for garnish (optional)
- Lime wedges for serving

Instructions:

1. Rinse the Rice:

- Rinse the rice under cold water until the water runs clear. This helps remove excess starch.

2. Cook the Rice:

- In a saucepan, combine the rinsed rice, coconut milk, water, sugar, and salt. Bring to a boil over medium-high heat.

3. Simmer:

- Reduce the heat to low, cover the saucepan with a tight-fitting lid, and simmer for 15-18 minutes or until the rice is cooked and has absorbed the liquid.

4. Fluff the Rice:

- Once the rice is cooked, fluff it with a fork to separate the grains.

5. Add Mango:

- Gently fold in the diced mango and shredded coconut (if using) into the cooked rice. The residual heat will slightly warm the mango.

6. Adjust Sweetness:

  - Taste the rice and adjust the sweetness by adding more sugar if desired. Mix well.

7. Garnish:

  - Garnish with fresh cilantro or mint leaves if you like.

8. Serve:

  - Serve the mango coconut rice warm, either as a side dish or a standalone dessert.

9. Lime Wedges:

  - Serve with lime wedges on the side. Squeezing a bit of lime juice over the rice can enhance the flavors.

10. Enjoy:

  - Enjoy this tropical and fragrant Mango Coconut Rice as a delightful accompaniment to your favorite dishes or as a sweet treat on its own.

This dish combines the sweetness of ripe mango with the creamy texture of coconut milk, creating a delicious and aromatic rice that is perfect for a variety of occasions.

Papaya Lime Sorbet Recipe

Ingredients:

- 2 cups ripe papaya, peeled, seeded, and diced
- 1/2 cup granulated sugar (adjust to taste)
- 1/4 cup fresh lime juice (about 2-3 limes)
- 1 teaspoon lime zest
- 1/2 cup water

Instructions:

1. Prepare the Papaya:

- Peel, seed, and dice the ripe papaya.

2. Make Simple Syrup:

- In a small saucepan, combine water and sugar. Heat over medium heat, stirring occasionally, until the sugar completely dissolves. Remove from heat and let the simple syrup cool.

3. Blend the Ingredients:

- In a blender or food processor, combine the diced papaya, fresh lime juice, lime zest, and the cooled simple syrup. Blend until you achieve a smooth puree.

4. Strain (Optional):

- If you prefer a smoother sorbet, you can strain the mixture through a fine mesh sieve to remove any pulp. This step is optional.

5. Chill the Mixture:

- Place the papaya and lime mixture in the refrigerator to chill for at least 2 hours.

6. Churn the Sorbet:

- Pour the chilled mixture into an ice cream maker and churn according to the manufacturer's instructions until it reaches a sorbet consistency.

7. Transfer to Freezer-Safe Container:

- Transfer the churned papaya lime sorbet into a freezer-safe container. Smooth the top with a spatula.

8. Freeze Until Firm:

- Freeze the sorbet for an additional 4-6 hours or overnight until it becomes firm.

9. Serve:

- Scoop the papaya lime sorbet into bowls or cones.

10. Garnish (Optional):

- Garnish with a slice of lime or a sprig of mint if desired.

11. Enjoy:

- Enjoy the refreshing and tropical flavor of homemade papaya lime sorbet!

This sorbet is a perfect way to enjoy the natural sweetness of papaya with a zesty kick from fresh lime. It's a delightful and light dessert for hot days or any time you crave a fruity treat.

Pomegranate Glazed Chicken Recipe

Ingredients:

For the Chicken:

- 4 boneless, skinless chicken breasts
- Salt and black pepper to taste
- 2 tablespoons olive oil

For the Pomegranate Glaze:

- 1 cup pomegranate juice
- 1/4 cup honey
- 2 tablespoons soy sauce
- 1 tablespoon Dijon mustard
- 2 cloves garlic, minced
- 1 teaspoon grated fresh ginger
- 1 tablespoon cornstarch (optional, for thickening)

For Garnish:

- Fresh pomegranate arils
- Chopped fresh parsley or cilantro

Instructions:

1. Preheat the Oven:

- Preheat your oven to 375°F (190°C).

2. Season the Chicken:

- Season the chicken breasts with salt and black pepper on both sides.

3. Sear the Chicken:

- In an oven-safe skillet, heat olive oil over medium-high heat. Sear the chicken breasts for 2-3 minutes on each side or until golden brown.

4. Make the Pomegranate Glaze:

    - In a bowl, whisk together pomegranate juice, honey, soy sauce, Dijon mustard, minced garlic, and grated ginger.

5. Glaze the Chicken:

    - Pour half of the pomegranate glaze over the seared chicken in the skillet.

6. Bake:

    - Transfer the skillet to the preheated oven and bake for 15-20 minutes or until the chicken is cooked through.

7. Baste with Glaze:

    - Baste the chicken with the remaining pomegranate glaze during the last 5 minutes of baking for a shiny finish.

8. Optional Thickening:

    - If you prefer a thicker glaze, mix cornstarch with a little water to create a slurry. Add it to the remaining glaze in the skillet and cook on the stovetop until it thickens.

9. Garnish:

    - Once out of the oven, garnish the glazed chicken with fresh pomegranate arils and chopped parsley or cilantro.

10. Serve:

    - Serve the pomegranate glazed chicken over rice, quinoa, or your favorite side dish.

11. Enjoy:

    - Enjoy the sweet and tangy flavor of this Pomegranate Glazed Chicken, a perfect combination of savory and fruity notes!

This dish is not only delicious but also visually stunning, making it a great choice for special occasions or a flavorful weeknight dinner.

Apple Cinnamon Oatmeal Recipe

Ingredients:

- 1 cup old-fashioned rolled oats
- 2 cups milk (dairy or plant-based)
- 1 large apple, peeled, cored, and diced
- 2 tablespoons maple syrup or honey
- 1 teaspoon ground cinnamon
- 1/4 teaspoon ground nutmeg
- Pinch of salt
- Optional toppings: sliced almonds, chopped walnuts, raisins, sliced bananas, or additional diced apples

Instructions:

1. Cook the Oats:

- In a saucepan, combine the rolled oats and milk. Bring to a gentle boil over medium heat, stirring occasionally.

2. Add Apples:

- Once the oats begin to simmer, add the diced apple, maple syrup or honey, ground cinnamon, ground nutmeg, and a pinch of salt.

3. Simmer:

- Reduce the heat to low and let the mixture simmer for about 5-7 minutes, or until the oats are cooked to your desired consistency. Stir occasionally to prevent sticking.

4. Adjust Sweetness:

- Taste the oatmeal and adjust the sweetness by adding more maple syrup or honey if needed. Stir to combine.

5. Serve:

- Once the oatmeal is cooked to your liking, remove the saucepan from the heat.

6. Optional Toppings:

- Serve the apple cinnamon oatmeal hot, and top with sliced almonds, chopped walnuts, raisins, sliced bananas, or additional diced apples for extra texture and flavor.

7. Enjoy:

- Enjoy a warm and comforting bowl of homemade apple cinnamon oatmeal, perfect for a wholesome breakfast or a cozy snack.

Note:

- You can customize the oatmeal by adjusting the consistency with more or less milk according to your preference.
- Experiment with different toppings to add variety and nutrition to your oatmeal.

Mango Coconut Rice Recipe

Ingredients:

- 1 cup basmati or jasmine rice
- 1 cup coconut milk
- 1 cup water
- 1 ripe mango, peeled, pitted, and diced
- 2 tablespoons shredded coconut (optional)
- 2 tablespoons sugar (adjust to taste)
- 1/4 teaspoon salt
- Fresh cilantro or mint for garnish (optional)
- Lime wedges for serving

Instructions:

1. Rinse the Rice:

- Rinse the rice under cold water until the water runs clear. This helps remove excess starch.

2. Cook the Rice:

- In a saucepan, combine the rinsed rice, coconut milk, water, sugar, and salt. Bring to a boil over medium-high heat.

3. Simmer:

- Reduce the heat to low, cover the saucepan with a tight-fitting lid, and simmer for 15-18 minutes or until the rice is cooked and has absorbed the liquid.

4. Fluff the Rice:

- Once the rice is cooked, fluff it with a fork to separate the grains.

5. Add Mango:

- Gently fold in the diced mango and shredded coconut (if using) into the cooked rice. The residual heat will slightly warm the mango.

6. Adjust Sweetness:

- Taste the rice and adjust the sweetness by adding more sugar if desired. Mix well.

7. Garnish:

- Garnish with fresh cilantro or mint leaves if you like.

8. Serve:

- Serve the mango coconut rice warm, either as a side dish or a standalone dessert.

9. Lime Wedges:

- Serve with lime wedges on the side. Squeezing a bit of lime juice over the rice can enhance the flavors.

10. Enjoy:

- Enjoy this tropical and fragrant Mango Coconut Rice as a delightful accompaniment to your favorite dishes or as a sweet treat on its own.

This dish combines the sweetness of ripe mango with the creamy texture of coconut milk, creating a delicious and aromatic rice that is perfect for a variety of occasions.

Papaya Lime Sorbet Recipe

Ingredients:

- 2 cups ripe papaya, peeled, seeded, and diced
- 1/2 cup granulated sugar (adjust to taste)
- 1/4 cup fresh lime juice (about 2-3 limes)
- 1 teaspoon lime zest
- 1/2 cup water

Instructions:

1. Prepare the Papaya:

- Peel, seed, and dice the ripe papaya.

2. Make Simple Syrup:

- In a small saucepan, combine water and sugar. Heat over medium heat, stirring occasionally, until the sugar completely dissolves. Remove from heat and let the simple syrup cool.

3. Blend the Ingredients:

- In a blender or food processor, combine the diced papaya, fresh lime juice, lime zest, and the cooled simple syrup. Blend until you achieve a smooth puree.

4. Strain (Optional):

- If you prefer a smoother sorbet, you can strain the mixture through a fine mesh sieve to remove any pulp. This step is optional.

5. Chill the Mixture:

- Place the papaya and lime mixture in the refrigerator to chill for at least 2 hours.

6. Churn the Sorbet:

- Pour the chilled mixture into an ice cream maker and churn according to the manufacturer's instructions until it reaches a sorbet consistency.

7. Transfer to Freezer-Safe Container:

- Transfer the churned papaya lime sorbet into a freezer-safe container. Smooth the top with a spatula.

8. Freeze Until Firm:

- Freeze the sorbet for an additional 4-6 hours or overnight until it becomes firm.

9. Serve:

- Scoop the papaya lime sorbet into bowls or cones.

10. Garnish (Optional):

- Garnish with a slice of lime or a sprig of mint if desired.

11. Enjoy:

- Enjoy the refreshing and tropical flavor of homemade papaya lime sorbet!

This sorbet is a perfect way to enjoy the natural sweetness of papaya with a zesty kick from fresh lime. It's a delightful and light dessert for hot days or any time you crave a fruity treat.

Banana Foster Crepes Recipe

Ingredients:

For the Crepes:

- 1 cup all-purpose flour
- 2 large eggs
- 1 1/4 cups milk
- 2 tablespoons melted butter
- 1 tablespoon sugar
- 1/4 teaspoon salt

For the Banana Foster Sauce:

- 4 ripe bananas, sliced
- 1/2 cup unsalted butter
- 1 cup brown sugar, packed
- 1/2 teaspoon ground cinnamon
- 1/4 cup dark rum (optional, for flambéing)
- Vanilla ice cream for serving

For Garnish:

- Chopped nuts (pecans or walnuts), optional

Instructions:

1. Prepare the Crepe Batter:

- In a blender, combine the flour, eggs, milk, melted butter, sugar, and salt. Blend until smooth. Allow the batter to rest for at least 30 minutes.

2. Cook the Crepes:

- Heat a non-stick skillet or crepe pan over medium heat. Pour a small amount of batter into the center of the pan, swirling it to spread the batter thinly. Cook for about 1-2 minutes per side or until lightly golden. Repeat until all crepes are cooked.

3. Make the Banana Foster Sauce:

- In a large skillet, melt the butter over medium heat. Add the sliced bananas, brown sugar, and ground cinnamon. Cook, stirring gently, until the bananas are coated and the sugar has melted, creating a caramel-like sauce.

4. Flambé (Optional):

- If you want to add a dramatic touch, carefully add the rum to the skillet and ignite with a long lighter. Allow the flame to subside naturally as the alcohol burns off. Be cautious and keep a lid nearby to smother the flame if needed.

5. Assemble the Crepes:

- Spoon the banana foster sauce onto each crepe, fold or roll the crepes, and place them on serving plates.

6. Serve:

- Serve the Banana Foster Crepes warm, topped with a scoop of vanilla ice cream and garnished with chopped nuts if desired.

7. Enjoy:

- Indulge in the rich and decadent flavors of Banana Foster Crepes for a delightful dessert experience.

This dessert combines the classic flavors of bananas foster with the delicate texture of crepes, creating a show-stopping treat perfect for special occasions or a luxurious weekend dessert.

Berry Stuffed French Toast Recipe

Ingredients:

For the Stuffed French Toast:

- 8 slices of thick bread (like brioche or challah)
- 4 ounces cream cheese, softened
- 1/2 cup mixed berries (strawberries, blueberries, raspberries)
- 4 large eggs
- 1 cup milk
- 1 teaspoon vanilla extract
- 1/4 teaspoon ground cinnamon
- Pinch of salt
- Butter or cooking spray for griddling

For the Berry Topping:

- 1 cup mixed berries
- 2 tablespoons maple syrup
- Powdered sugar for dusting (optional)

Instructions:

1. Prepare the Cream Cheese Filling:

- In a bowl, mix the softened cream cheese until smooth. Fold in the mixed berries, combining well. Set aside.

2. Make the Berry Topping:

- In a small saucepan, combine 1 cup of mixed berries and maple syrup. Heat over medium heat until the berries release their juices and the mixture thickens slightly. Remove from heat.

3. Create the Stuffed French Toast:

- Lay out 8 slices of bread and spread the cream cheese and berry mixture onto 4 slices. Top each with another slice to create a sandwich.

4. Whisk the Egg Mixture:

- In a shallow dish, whisk together eggs, milk, vanilla extract, ground cinnamon, and a pinch of salt.

5. Dip and Cook:

- Dip each stuffed sandwich into the egg mixture, ensuring both sides are well-coated.

6. Griddle or Pan Fry:

- In a griddle or large skillet over medium heat, melt butter or use cooking spray. Cook the stuffed French toast sandwiches until golden brown on both sides and the cream cheese filling is softened.

7. Serve:

- Place the stuffed French toast on serving plates.

8. Top with Berry Sauce:

- Spoon the berry topping over the stuffed French toast.

9. Dust with Powdered Sugar (Optional):

- If desired, dust with powdered sugar for an extra touch of sweetness.

10. Enjoy:

- Serve the Berry Stuffed French Toast warm and enjoy a delightful breakfast or brunch treat.

This Berry Stuffed French Toast is a delicious combination of creamy, fruity goodness encased in golden and crispy bread. It's a perfect way to elevate your breakfast or brunch experience.

Honey Lime Grilled Pineapple Recipe

Ingredients:

- 1 ripe pineapple, peeled, cored, and sliced into rings or wedges
- 1/4 cup honey
- 2 tablespoons fresh lime juice
- 1 teaspoon lime zest
- 1 tablespoon melted butter (optional, for brushing on the grill)
- Fresh mint leaves for garnish (optional)
- Vanilla ice cream or whipped cream for serving (optional)

Instructions:

1. Preheat the Grill:

- Preheat your grill to medium-high heat.

2. Prepare the Honey Lime Marinade:

- In a bowl, whisk together the honey, fresh lime juice, and lime zest to create the marinade.

3. Brush the Grill Grates:

- Lightly brush the grill grates with oil or use a non-stick grilling spray to prevent the pineapple from sticking.

4. Marinate the Pineapple:

- Dip each pineapple slice into the honey lime marinade, ensuring they are well-coated. You can also use a basting brush to apply the marinade.

5. Grill the Pineapple:

- Place the marinated pineapple slices on the preheated grill. Grill for 2-3 minutes per side or until you see grill marks and the pineapple has caramelized slightly.

6. Baste with Marinade:

- As the pineapple cooks, you can baste it with more of the honey lime marinade for added flavor.

7. Optional Butter Brush (for Extra Flavor):

    - In the last minute of grilling, you can brush the pineapple slices with melted butter for an extra layer of richness. This step is optional.

8. Remove from Grill:

    - Once the pineapple is grilled to your liking, remove it from the grill and place it on a serving platter.

9. Garnish and Serve:

    - Garnish the grilled pineapple with fresh mint leaves if desired. Serve it as is, or pair it with a scoop of vanilla ice cream or a dollop of whipped cream for a delightful dessert.

10. Enjoy:

    - Enjoy the sweet and tangy flavor of Honey Lime Grilled Pineapple as a refreshing and easy-to-make dessert or side dish.

This grilled pineapple recipe is perfect for summer gatherings, barbecues, or simply as a delicious treat to satisfy your sweet cravings.

Blackberry Balsamic Chicken Recipe

Ingredients:

For the Chicken:

- 4 boneless, skinless chicken breasts
- Salt and black pepper to taste
- 2 tablespoons olive oil

For the Blackberry Balsamic Sauce:

- 1 cup fresh blackberries
- 2 tablespoons balsamic vinegar
- 2 tablespoons honey
- 1 tablespoon Dijon mustard
- 2 cloves garlic, minced
- Salt and black pepper to taste

For Garnish:

- Fresh basil or mint leaves, chopped (optional)

Instructions:

1. Preheat the Oven:

- Preheat your oven to 375°F (190°C).

2. Season the Chicken:

- Season the chicken breasts with salt and black pepper on both sides.

3. Sear the Chicken:

- In an oven-safe skillet, heat olive oil over medium-high heat. Sear the chicken breasts for 2-3 minutes on each side or until golden brown.

4. Make the Blackberry Balsamic Sauce:

- In a blender or food processor, blend the fresh blackberries until smooth. Strain the puree through a fine mesh sieve to remove the seeds, collecting the juice.

5. Combine Ingredients:

    - In a bowl, whisk together the blackberry puree, balsamic vinegar, honey, Dijon mustard, minced garlic, salt, and black pepper.

6. Glaze the Chicken:

    - Pour the blackberry balsamic sauce over the seared chicken in the skillet.

7. Bake:

    - Transfer the skillet to the preheated oven and bake for 20-25 minutes or until the chicken is cooked through.

8. Baste with Sauce:

    - Baste the chicken with the sauce from the skillet during the last 5 minutes of baking for extra flavor.

9. Garnish:

    - Once out of the oven, garnish the chicken with chopped fresh basil or mint leaves if desired.

10. Serve:

    - Serve the Blackberry Balsamic Chicken over rice, quinoa, or your favorite side.

11. Enjoy:

    - Enjoy the succulent and flavorful Blackberry Balsamic Chicken as a delicious and unique main course.

This dish offers a perfect balance of sweet and tangy flavors, and the vibrant color of the blackberry balsamic sauce adds a touch of elegance to your dinner table.

Apricot Almond Energy Bites Recipe

Ingredients:

- 1 cup dried apricots, unsweetened
- 1 cup almonds, raw or roasted
- 1/2 cup rolled oats
- 2 tablespoons chia seeds
- 1/4 cup honey or maple syrup
- 1 teaspoon vanilla extract
- A pinch of salt
- Shredded coconut or chopped almonds for coating (optional)

Instructions:

1. Prepare Ingredients:

- If the apricots are very dry, soak them in warm water for about 10-15 minutes to soften. Drain before using.

2. Blend Ingredients:

- In a food processor, combine dried apricots, almonds, rolled oats, chia seeds, honey or maple syrup, vanilla extract, and a pinch of salt. Blend until the mixture comes together into a sticky, uniform texture.

3. Check Consistency:

- Check the consistency of the mixture. If it seems too dry and doesn't hold together well when pressed, you can add a bit more honey or maple syrup and blend again.

4. Form Energy Bites:

- Scoop out portions of the mixture and roll them between your hands to form bite-sized energy balls. If the mixture is sticky, lightly wetting your hands can make it easier to handle.

5. Optional Coating:

- If desired, roll the energy bites in shredded coconut or chopped almonds for an extra layer of flavor and texture.

6. Chill:

- Place the energy bites on a plate or tray and refrigerate for at least 30 minutes to firm up.

7. Store:

- Once chilled, transfer the apricot almond energy bites to an airtight container and store in the refrigerator for longer shelf life.

8. Enjoy:

- Enjoy these nutritious and delicious Apricot Almond Energy Bites as a quick snack or energy boost throughout the day.

These energy bites are not only tasty but also packed with the goodness of dried apricots, almonds, oats, and chia seeds. They make for a convenient and healthy snack option, providing a natural source of energy.

Classic Strawberry Shortcake Recipe

Ingredients:

For the Shortcakes:

- 2 cups all-purpose flour
- 1/4 cup granulated sugar
- 1 tablespoon baking powder
- 1/2 teaspoon salt
- 1/2 cup unsalted butter, cold and cut into small pieces
- 2/3 cup milk
- 1 teaspoon vanilla extract

For the Strawberries:

- 4 cups fresh strawberries, hulled and sliced
- 1/4 cup granulated sugar (adjust to taste)
- 1 teaspoon balsamic vinegar (optional, for depth of flavor)

For the Whipped Cream:

- 1 cup heavy cream
- 2 tablespoons powdered sugar
- 1 teaspoon vanilla extract

Instructions:

1. Preheat the Oven:

- Preheat your oven to 425°F (220°C). Line a baking sheet with parchment paper.

2. Make the Shortcakes:

- In a large bowl, whisk together flour, sugar, baking powder, and salt. Add the cold, cubed butter and use a pastry cutter or your fingers to cut the butter into the dry ingredients until the mixture resembles coarse crumbs.
- Pour in the milk and vanilla extract. Stir until just combined. Do not overmix.

- Turn the dough out onto a floured surface. Pat it into a rectangle about 1-inch thick. Use a round biscuit cutter to cut out shortcakes and place them on the prepared baking sheet.

3. Bake the Shortcakes:

- Bake in the preheated oven for 12-15 minutes or until the shortcakes are golden brown. Allow them to cool on a wire rack.

4. Prepare the Strawberries:

- In a bowl, combine sliced strawberries with sugar. If desired, add balsamic vinegar for a depth of flavor. Toss gently and let the strawberries macerate for at least 15 minutes.

5. Make the Whipped Cream:

- In a separate bowl, whip the heavy cream, powdered sugar, and vanilla extract until stiff peaks form.

6. Assemble the Strawberry Shortcakes:

- Once the shortcakes have cooled, slice them in half horizontally. Spoon a generous amount of macerated strawberries onto the bottom half, add a dollop of whipped cream, and top with the other half of the shortcake.

7. Serve:

- Serve the strawberry shortcakes immediately. Optionally, drizzle extra strawberry juices over the top for added flavor.

8. Enjoy:

- Enjoy this classic Strawberry Shortcake, a delightful and timeless dessert that celebrates the sweetness of fresh strawberries and fluffy shortcakes!

Mango Avocado Salsa Recipe

Ingredients:

- 2 ripe mangos, peeled, pitted, and diced
- 1 ripe avocado, peeled, pitted, and diced
- 1/2 red onion, finely diced
- 1 jalapeño pepper, seeds and membranes removed, finely chopped
- 1/4 cup fresh cilantro, chopped
- Juice of 2 limes
- Salt and pepper to taste

Instructions:

1. Prepare the Mango and Avocado:

- Peel, pit, and dice the ripe mangos and avocado. Ensure they are cut into bite-sized pieces.

2. Dice the Red Onion:

- Finely dice the red onion. Adjust the quantity according to your preference.

3. Prepare the Jalapeño:

- Finely chop the jalapeño pepper after removing the seeds and membranes. Adjust the amount to your desired level of spiciness.

4. Chop the Cilantro:

- Chop the fresh cilantro finely. You can adjust the amount based on your taste preferences.

5. Combine Ingredients:

- In a mixing bowl, combine the diced mango, diced avocado, finely diced red onion, chopped jalapeño, and cilantro.

6. Add Lime Juice:

- Squeeze the juice of two limes over the mixture. Lime juice adds a bright and citrusy flavor to the salsa.

7. Season with Salt and Pepper:

- Season the salsa with salt and pepper to taste. Mix all the ingredients gently to combine.

8. Let It Rest:

- Allow the salsa to rest for about 10-15 minutes before serving. This allows the flavors to meld together.

9. Adjust Seasoning (Optional):

- Taste the salsa and adjust the seasoning if necessary. You can add more lime juice, salt, or pepper according to your preference.

10. Serve:

- Serve the Mango Avocado Salsa as a topping for grilled chicken, fish, tacos, or as a refreshing dip with tortilla chips.

11. Enjoy:

- Enjoy the vibrant and flavorful Mango Avocado Salsa as a delicious and tropical addition to your meals!

This salsa is not only delicious but also versatile, bringing a burst of freshness and tropical flair to your dishes. It's perfect for summer gatherings or anytime you want a refreshing and wholesome accompaniment.

Raspberry Chocolate Chip Muffins Recipe

Ingredients:

- 2 cups all-purpose flour
- 1/2 cup granulated sugar
- 1/4 cup light brown sugar, packed
- 2 teaspoons baking powder
- 1/2 teaspoon baking soda
- 1/4 teaspoon salt
- 1 cup buttermilk
- 1/2 cup unsalted butter, melted and cooled
- 2 large eggs
- 1 teaspoon vanilla extract
- 1 cup fresh raspberries
- 1/2 cup chocolate chips (semi-sweet or dark chocolate)

Instructions:

1. Preheat the Oven:

- Preheat your oven to 375°F (190°C). Line a muffin tin with paper liners or grease the cups.

2. Mix Dry Ingredients:

- In a large bowl, whisk together the flour, granulated sugar, brown sugar, baking powder, baking soda, and salt.

3. Mix Wet Ingredients:

- In another bowl, whisk together the buttermilk, melted butter, eggs, and vanilla extract until well combined.

4. Combine Wet and Dry Ingredients:

- Pour the wet ingredients into the dry ingredients. Stir until just combined. Do not overmix; a few lumps are okay.

5. Add Raspberries and Chocolate Chips:

- Gently fold in the fresh raspberries and chocolate chips into the batter.

6. Fill Muffin Cups:

    - Using a spoon or an ice cream scoop, divide the batter evenly among the muffin cups, filling each about 2/3 full.

7. Bake:

    - Bake in the preheated oven for 18-20 minutes or until a toothpick inserted into the center comes out clean or with a few moist crumbs.

8. Cool:

    - Allow the muffins to cool in the tin for 5 minutes, then transfer them to a wire rack to cool completely.

9. Enjoy:

    - Enjoy these Raspberry Chocolate Chip Muffins as a delightful treat for breakfast or as a sweet snack!

These muffins combine the tartness of fresh raspberries with the sweetness of chocolate chips, creating a perfect balance of flavors. They are great for brunches, picnics, or whenever you're craving a delicious homemade muffin.

Citrus Salad with Mint Recipe

Ingredients:

For the Salad:

- 3 oranges (mix of varieties like navel and blood oranges)
- 2 grapefruits (pink or red grapefruits work well)
- 1 lime
- 1 tablespoon honey or maple syrup (optional, for drizzling)
- Fresh mint leaves, for garnish

For the Mint Syrup:

- 1/4 cup fresh mint leaves, finely chopped
- 1/4 cup granulated sugar
- 1/4 cup water

Instructions:

1. Segment the Citrus:

- Cut the top and bottom off each orange and grapefruit to expose the fruit. Using a sharp knife, remove the peel and pith by following the curve of the fruit. Hold the fruit over a bowl and carefully cut along the membranes to release individual citrus segments (supremes). Repeat this process for all citrus fruits.

2. Collect Citrus Juice:

- Squeeze the membranes over the bowl to collect any remaining juice. Reserve this juice for later use.

3. Prepare Mint Syrup:

- In a small saucepan, combine the chopped mint leaves, granulated sugar, and water. Heat over medium heat, stirring occasionally, until the sugar dissolves. Simmer for 2-3 minutes, then remove from heat. Allow the mint syrup to cool.

4. Assemble the Salad:

- Arrange the citrus segments on a serving platter or individual plates.

5. Drizzle with Mint Syrup:

    - Drizzle the mint syrup over the citrus segments. If you prefer added sweetness, you can also drizzle honey or maple syrup at this stage.

6. Garnish with Mint Leaves:

    - Scatter fresh mint leaves over the citrus salad for a burst of flavor and a decorative touch.

7. Optional: Chill Before Serving:

    - You can refrigerate the citrus salad for 30 minutes to an hour before serving for a refreshing and chilled experience.

8. Serve:

    - Serve the Citrus Salad with Mint as a vibrant and refreshing side dish or dessert.

9. Enjoy:

    - Enjoy the burst of citrusy flavors complemented by the subtle sweetness of mint syrup in this delightful and healthy salad!

This Citrus Salad with Mint is not only visually appealing but also a perfect combination of sweet, tangy, and minty flavors. It's a great addition to your summer menu or any time you crave a refreshing and light dish.

Plum Ginger Jam Recipe

Ingredients:

- 2 pounds (about 6 cups) ripe plums, pitted and chopped
- 1 1/2 cups granulated sugar
- 2 tablespoons fresh ginger, grated
- 1 tablespoon lemon juice
- 1 teaspoon lemon zest
- 1/2 teaspoon ground cinnamon (optional)

Instructions:

1. Prepare the Plums:

- Wash, pit, and chop the ripe plums into small, bite-sized pieces.

2. Grate the Fresh Ginger:

- Peel and grate the fresh ginger using a fine grater or zester.

3. Combine Ingredients:

- In a large, heavy-bottomed pot, combine the chopped plums, granulated sugar, grated ginger, lemon juice, lemon zest, and ground cinnamon if using. Stir well to combine.

4. Cook on Medium Heat:

- Place the pot over medium heat and bring the mixture to a gentle boil. Stir frequently to prevent sticking.

5. Simmer and Stir:

- Once it reaches a boil, reduce the heat to low and let the mixture simmer. Continue to stir frequently to prevent the jam from burning at the bottom.

6. Test for Jam Consistency:

- After about 30-40 minutes of simmering, perform the "wrinkle test" to check the consistency. Place a small amount of the jam on a cold plate, let it sit for a moment, and then push it with your finger. If it wrinkles and holds its shape, the jam is ready.

7. Adjust Flavor (Optional):

- Taste the jam and adjust the flavor if needed. You can add more sugar for sweetness or more lemon juice for acidity.

8. Remove from Heat:

- Once the jam reaches the desired consistency, remove it from heat.

9. Cool and Store:

- Allow the plum ginger jam to cool slightly before transferring it into sterilized jars. Seal the jars and let them cool completely.

10. Store in the Refrigerator:

- Store the plum ginger jam in the refrigerator for up to several weeks.

11. Enjoy:

- Enjoy the delightful combination of plum and ginger flavors in this homemade jam on toast, as a topping for desserts, or in various culinary creations!

This Plum Ginger Jam offers a unique and flavorful twist on traditional fruit jams. The warmth of ginger complements the sweetness of plums, creating a versatile condiment that can be enjoyed in a variety of ways.

Apple Pecan Salad Recipe

Ingredients:

For the Salad:

- 6 cups mixed salad greens (e.g., spinach, arugula, and romaine)
- 2 medium apples, thinly sliced (use your favorite variety)
- 1 cup chopped celery
- 1 cup candied or glazed pecans
- 1/2 cup crumbled feta cheese (optional)
- 1/4 cup thinly sliced red onion

For the Dressing:

- 1/4 cup apple cider vinegar
- 1/4 cup extra-virgin olive oil
- 2 tablespoons Dijon mustard
- 1 tablespoon honey
- Salt and pepper to taste

Instructions:

1. Prepare the Salad Greens:

    - In a large salad bowl, combine the mixed greens, thinly sliced apples, chopped celery, candied pecans, crumbled feta cheese (if using), and thinly sliced red onion.

2. Make the Dressing:

    - In a small bowl, whisk together the apple cider vinegar, extra-virgin olive oil, Dijon mustard, honey, salt, and pepper until well combined.

3. Dress the Salad:

    - Drizzle the dressing over the salad ingredients. Toss gently to coat the salad evenly with the dressing.

4. Optional: Chill Before Serving:

- If desired, refrigerate the salad for 15-30 minutes before serving to allow the flavors to meld and the salad to cool slightly.

5. Serve:

- Transfer the salad to individual plates or a serving platter.

6. Garnish (Optional):

- Garnish with additional pecans, feta cheese, or a sprinkle of fresh herbs if desired.

7. Enjoy:

- Serve the Apple Pecan Salad as a refreshing and flavorful side dish or add grilled chicken or shrimp to make it a complete meal.

This salad combines the crispness of apples, the crunchiness of pecans, and the sweetness of candied pecans, creating a delightful medley of flavors and textures. The honey Dijon dressing adds a perfect balance to this delicious and nutritious salad.

Peach Barbecue Chicken Recipe

Ingredients:

For the Peach Barbecue Sauce:

- 2 cups fresh or frozen peaches, peeled and diced
- 1/2 cup ketchup
- 1/4 cup brown sugar
- 2 tablespoons apple cider vinegar
- 1 tablespoon Dijon mustard
- 1 tablespoon soy sauce
- 1 teaspoon Worcestershire sauce
- 1 teaspoon smoked paprika
- 1/2 teaspoon garlic powder
- Salt and black pepper to taste

For the Chicken:

- 4 boneless, skinless chicken breasts
- Salt and black pepper to taste
- Olive oil for grilling

Instructions:

1. Prepare the Peach Barbecue Sauce:

- In a blender or food processor, combine the diced peaches, ketchup, brown sugar, apple cider vinegar, Dijon mustard, soy sauce, Worcestershire sauce, smoked paprika, garlic powder, salt, and black pepper. Blend until smooth.

2. Simmer the Sauce:

- Transfer the peach mixture to a saucepan and bring it to a simmer over medium heat. Reduce the heat to low and let it simmer for 15-20 minutes, stirring occasionally, until the sauce thickens and the flavors meld. Adjust the seasoning if needed.

3. Prepare the Chicken:

- Season the chicken breasts with salt and black pepper.

4. Grill the Chicken:

    - Preheat the grill to medium-high heat. Brush the chicken breasts with olive oil to prevent sticking.
    - Grill the chicken for about 6-8 minutes per side, or until the internal temperature reaches 165°F (74°C) and the chicken is cooked through.

5. Glaze with Peach Barbecue Sauce:

    - In the last few minutes of grilling, brush the chicken breasts generously with the peach barbecue sauce, allowing it to caramelize and create a flavorful glaze.

6. Serve:

    - Transfer the grilled Peach Barbecue Chicken to a serving platter.

7. Drizzle with More Sauce (Optional):

    - If desired, drizzle extra peach barbecue sauce over the chicken before serving.

8. Garnish (Optional):

    - Garnish with chopped fresh herbs, such as parsley or cilantro, for a burst of freshness.

9. Enjoy:

    - Serve the Peach Barbecue Chicken with your favorite side dishes and enjoy a delicious and fruity twist on classic barbecue chicken.

This Peach Barbecue Chicken is a perfect dish for summer grilling, offering a balance of smoky, sweet, and tangy flavors. The peach barbecue sauce adds a unique and delightful twist to your grilled chicken.

Mango Coconut Chia Pudding Recipe

Ingredients:

For the Chia Pudding:

- 1/4 cup chia seeds
- 1 cup coconut milk (canned or homemade)
- 2 tablespoons maple syrup or honey
- 1/2 teaspoon vanilla extract

For the Mango Layer:

- 1 ripe mango, peeled and diced
- 1 tablespoon lime juice
- 1 tablespoon shredded coconut (optional, for garnish)

Instructions:

1. Make the Chia Pudding:

- In a bowl, whisk together the chia seeds, coconut milk, maple syrup or honey, and vanilla extract. Ensure that the chia seeds are well combined with the liquid to avoid clumping.

2. Let It Set:

- Cover the bowl and refrigerate the chia pudding mixture for at least 4 hours or overnight. This allows the chia seeds to absorb the liquid and create a pudding-like consistency.

3. Blend the Mango Layer:

- In a blender or food processor, blend the diced mango and lime juice until smooth.

4. Assemble the Pudding Cups:

- Take serving cups or jars. Layer the chia pudding and mango puree in alternating layers.

5. Optional: Create Swirls:

- Use a spoon to create swirls or patterns between the chia pudding and mango layers for an aesthetic touch.

6. Garnish:

- Optionally, sprinkle shredded coconut over the top for added texture and flavor.

7. Chill (Optional):

- Place the assembled pudding cups back in the refrigerator for a little while if you prefer a chilled dessert.

8. Serve:

- Serve the Mango Coconut Chia Pudding cups chilled.

9. Enjoy:

- Enjoy this tropical and refreshing Mango Coconut Chia Pudding as a nutritious breakfast, snack, or dessert!

This chia pudding with layers of mango and coconut is not only delicious but also loaded with health benefits. Chia seeds provide fiber and omega-3 fatty acids, while mango adds natural sweetness and a burst of tropical flavor. It's a delightful and satisfying treat that's easy to prepare.

Blueberry Balsamic Glazed Salmon Recipe

Ingredients:

For the Blueberry Balsamic Glaze:

- 1 cup fresh or frozen blueberries
- 3 tablespoons balsamic vinegar
- 2 tablespoons honey
- 1 tablespoon Dijon mustard
- 1 clove garlic, minced
- Salt and black pepper to taste

For the Salmon:

- 4 salmon fillets
- Salt and black pepper to taste
- 1 tablespoon olive oil
- Fresh lemon wedges for serving
- Fresh parsley for garnish (optional)

Instructions:

1. Prepare the Blueberry Balsamic Glaze:

- In a saucepan, combine blueberries, balsamic vinegar, honey, Dijon mustard, minced garlic, salt, and black pepper. Bring the mixture to a simmer over medium heat.
- Reduce the heat to low and let it simmer for 10-15 minutes, stirring occasionally, until the blueberries break down, and the sauce thickens. Adjust the sweetness and seasoning to your liking. Set aside.

2. Preheat the Oven:

- Preheat your oven to 400°F (200°C).

3. Season the Salmon:

- Season the salmon fillets with salt and black pepper.

4. Sear the Salmon:

- In an oven-safe skillet, heat olive oil over medium-high heat. Sear the salmon fillets, skin side down, for 2-3 minutes until the skin is crispy.

5. Glaze the Salmon:

- Brush the blueberry balsamic glaze over the tops of the salmon fillets.

6. Bake:

- Transfer the skillet to the preheated oven and bake for 10-12 minutes or until the salmon is cooked through and flakes easily with a fork.

7. Glaze Again (Optional):

- If desired, you can brush additional glaze over the salmon during the last few minutes of baking for extra flavor.

8. Serve:

- Carefully remove the skillet from the oven. Serve the blueberry balsamic glazed salmon on plates.

9. Garnish (Optional):

- Garnish with fresh parsley and serve with lemon wedges.

10. Enjoy:

- Enjoy this flavorful and unique Blueberry Balsamic Glazed Salmon as a delicious and healthful main course!

The combination of blueberry and balsamic creates a sweet and tangy glaze that pairs perfectly with the richness of salmon. This dish is not only tasty but also a feast for the eyes, making it an excellent choice for a special dinner or a celebration.

Pineapple Upside-Down Cake Recipe

Ingredients:

For the Topping:

- 1/2 cup unsalted butter
- 1 cup packed brown sugar
- 1 can pineapple rings (about 8-10 rings), drained
- Maraschino cherries, for decoration

For the Cake Batter:

- 1 and 1/2 cups all-purpose flour
- 1 and 1/2 teaspoons baking powder
- 1/2 teaspoon baking soda
- 1/4 teaspoon salt
- 1/2 cup unsalted butter, softened
- 1 cup granulated sugar
- 2 large eggs
- 1 teaspoon vanilla extract
- 3/4 cup buttermilk

Instructions:

1. Preheat the Oven:

- Preheat your oven to 350°F (175°C). Grease a 9-inch round cake pan.

2. Prepare the Topping:

- In a small saucepan, melt the 1/2 cup of butter over low heat. Add the brown sugar and stir until it is completely dissolved. Pour this mixture into the bottom of the greased cake pan.
- Arrange the pineapple rings over the brown sugar mixture. Place a maraschino cherry in the center of each pineapple ring.

3. Make the Cake Batter:

- In a medium bowl, whisk together the flour, baking powder, baking soda, and salt.

- In a separate large bowl, cream together the softened butter and granulated sugar until light and fluffy. Add the eggs one at a time, beating well after each addition. Stir in the vanilla extract.
- Gradually add the dry ingredients to the wet ingredients, alternating with the buttermilk. Begin and end with the dry ingredients. Mix until just combined.

4. Pour Batter Over Pineapple:

- Pour the cake batter over the arranged pineapple and smooth the top with a spatula.

5. Bake:

- Bake in the preheated oven for 40-45 minutes or until a toothpick inserted into the center of the cake comes out clean.

6. Cool and Invert:

- Allow the cake to cool in the pan for 10-15 minutes. Run a knife around the edge of the cake to loosen it. Invert the cake onto a serving plate.

7. Serve:

- Serve the Pineapple Upside-Down Cake warm or at room temperature. Enjoy the delicious blend of caramelized pineapple and moist cake!

This classic Pineapple Upside-Down Cake is a timeless dessert that's both visually appealing and irresistibly delicious. It's perfect for special occasions or as a sweet treat to enjoy with family and friends.

Cinnamon Apple Chips Recipe

Ingredients:

- 4-5 large apples (use a sweet variety like Honeycrisp or Fuji)
- 1-2 tablespoons ground cinnamon
- 1-2 tablespoons granulated sugar (optional, depending on the sweetness of the apples)

Instructions:

1. Preheat the Oven:

- Preheat your oven to 200°F (95°C). Line two baking sheets with parchment paper.

2. Prepare the Apples:

- Wash and core the apples. Thinly slice the apples into uniform slices, about 1/8-inch thick. You can use a sharp knife or a mandoline for precision.

3. Cinnamon Sugar Mixture:

- In a bowl, mix the ground cinnamon with granulated sugar if using. Adjust the sugar quantity based on your preference and the sweetness of the apples.

4. Coat the Apple Slices:

- Place the apple slices in a large bowl. Sprinkle the cinnamon sugar mixture over the apple slices and toss gently to coat each slice evenly.

5. Arrange on Baking Sheets:

- Lay the coated apple slices in a single layer on the prepared baking sheets, ensuring they are not touching each other.

6. Bake Low and Slow:

- Bake in the preheated oven for 2-3 hours, flipping the apple slices halfway through the baking time. The low temperature allows the apples to dehydrate and become crispy.

7. Check for Crispiness:

- Check the apple slices for crispiness. They should be firm and dry, but not overly browned.

8. Cool:

- Allow the cinnamon apple chips to cool completely on the baking sheets. They will continue to crisp up as they cool.

9. Store:

- Once completely cooled, transfer the cinnamon apple chips to an airtight container or zip-top bag for storage. They should be stored in a cool, dry place.

10. Enjoy:

- Enjoy these delicious and healthy Cinnamon Apple Chips as a wholesome snack or as a crunchy topping for yogurt, oatmeal, or desserts.

These homemade cinnamon apple chips are a delightful alternative to store-bought snacks, providing a naturally sweet and crunchy treat. They're not only delicious but also a nutritious option for satisfying your sweet tooth.

Lemon Raspberry Thumbprint Cookies Recipe

Ingredients:

For the Cookies:

- 1 cup unsalted butter, softened
- 2/3 cup granulated sugar
- 1 large egg
- 1 teaspoon vanilla extract
- Zest of 1 lemon
- 2 cups all-purpose flour
- 1/2 teaspoon salt

For the Filling:

- 1/2 cup raspberry jam or preserves

For the Glaze (Optional):

- 1 cup powdered sugar
- 2 tablespoons fresh lemon juice
- 1 teaspoon lemon zest

Instructions:

1. Preheat the Oven:

- Preheat your oven to 350°F (175°C). Line two baking sheets with parchment paper.

2. Make the Cookie Dough:

- In a large bowl, cream together the softened butter and granulated sugar until light and fluffy. Add the egg, vanilla extract, and lemon zest. Mix until well combined.
- In a separate bowl, whisk together the flour and salt. Gradually add the dry ingredients to the wet ingredients, mixing until just combined.

3. Form Cookie Dough Balls:

- Scoop tablespoon-sized portions of cookie dough and roll them into balls. Place the cookie dough balls onto the prepared baking sheets, leaving space between each.

4. Create Thumbprints:

- Use your thumb or the back of a teaspoon to make an indentation in the center of each cookie. Ensure not to press too hard to avoid cracking.

5. Add Raspberry Filling:

- Spoon a small amount (about 1/2 teaspoon) of raspberry jam into the indentation of each cookie.

6. Bake:

- Bake in the preheated oven for 12-15 minutes or until the edges of the cookies are lightly golden.

7. Cool:

- Allow the cookies to cool on the baking sheets for a few minutes before transferring them to a wire rack to cool completely.

8. Make the Glaze (Optional):

- In a small bowl, whisk together powdered sugar, fresh lemon juice, and lemon zest until you have a smooth glaze.

9. Glaze the Cookies:

- Once the cookies are completely cooled, drizzle the lemon glaze over the top using a spoon or a piping bag.

10. Let the Glaze Set:

- Allow the glaze to set before serving or storing the cookies.

11. Enjoy:

- Enjoy these delightful Lemon Raspberry Thumbprint Cookies with a perfect balance of citrusy lemon and sweet raspberry flavors!

These thumbprint cookies are not only visually appealing but also a burst of flavor in every bite. The combination of lemony cookies and raspberry jam creates a delightful treat that's perfect for various occasions.

Gingered Pear Muffins Recipe

Ingredients:

Dry Ingredients:

- 2 cups all-purpose flour
- 1 teaspoon baking powder
- 1/2 teaspoon baking soda
- 1/2 teaspoon salt
- 1 teaspoon ground ginger
- 1/2 teaspoon ground cinnamon

Wet Ingredients:

- 1/2 cup unsalted butter, melted and cooled
- 1/2 cup granulated sugar
- 1/2 cup brown sugar, packed
- 2 large eggs
- 1 teaspoon vanilla extract

Additional Ingredients:

- 1 cup ripe pears, peeled and diced
- 1/4 cup crystallized ginger, finely chopped (optional, for added ginger flavor and texture)

Instructions:

1. Preheat the Oven:

- Preheat your oven to 375°F (190°C). Line a muffin tin with paper liners or grease the cups.

2. Prepare the Dry Ingredients:

- In a large bowl, whisk together the flour, baking powder, baking soda, salt, ground ginger, and ground cinnamon. Set aside.

3. Mix the Wet Ingredients:

- In another bowl, whisk together the melted butter, granulated sugar, brown sugar, eggs, and vanilla extract until well combined.

4. Combine Wet and Dry Ingredients:

- Pour the wet ingredients into the bowl of dry ingredients. Stir until just combined. Do not overmix.

5. Add Pears and Crystallized Ginger:

- Gently fold in the diced pears and crystallized ginger (if using) into the muffin batter.

6. Fill Muffin Cups:

- Spoon the batter into the prepared muffin cups, filling each about 2/3 full.

7. Bake:

- Bake in the preheated oven for 18-20 minutes or until a toothpick inserted into the center of a muffin comes out clean or with a few moist crumbs.

8. Cool:

- Allow the muffins to cool in the tin for 5 minutes, then transfer them to a wire rack to cool completely.

9. Enjoy:

- Enjoy these delicious and moist Gingered Pear Muffins as a delightful breakfast or snack!

The combination of ginger and sweet pears creates a flavorful and aromatic muffin that is perfect for fall or any time you want a cozy and comforting treat. The addition of crystallized ginger adds a delightful burst of ginger flavor and a touch of sweetness.

Mixed Berry Cobb Salad Recipe

Ingredients:

For the Salad:

- 6 cups mixed salad greens (e.g., spinach, arugula, romaine)
- 1 cup cooked and diced chicken breast
- 1 cup fresh strawberries, hulled and sliced
- 1 cup fresh blueberries
- 1 cup fresh raspberries
- 1 cup crumbled feta cheese
- 1/2 cup chopped pecans or walnuts
- 4 hard-boiled eggs, sliced

For the Balsamic Vinaigrette:

- 1/4 cup balsamic vinegar
- 1/2 cup extra-virgin olive oil
- 1 tablespoon Dijon mustard
- 1 clove garlic, minced
- Salt and pepper to taste

Instructions:

1. Prepare the Salad Greens:

- In a large salad bowl, combine the mixed greens, creating a base for the Cobb salad.

2. Arrange the Ingredients:

- Arrange the diced chicken breast, sliced strawberries, blueberries, raspberries, crumbled feta cheese, chopped nuts, and sliced hard-boiled eggs on top of the salad greens.

3. Make the Balsamic Vinaigrette:

- In a small bowl or jar, whisk together the balsamic vinegar, extra-virgin olive oil, Dijon mustard, minced garlic, salt, and pepper until well combined. Adjust the seasoning to taste.

4. Drizzle with Dressing:

- Drizzle the balsamic vinaigrette over the mixed berry Cobb salad.

5. Toss Gently:

- Gently toss the salad to ensure the ingredients are evenly coated with the dressing.

6. Serve:

- Serve the Mixed Berry Cobb Salad on individual plates or a large platter.

7. Enjoy:

- Enjoy this refreshing and colorful salad as a wholesome and flavorful meal!

This Mixed Berry Cobb Salad offers a delightful combination of sweet berries, savory chicken, and the richness of feta cheese. The balsamic vinaigrette ties all the flavors together, creating a delicious and satisfying salad that's perfect for a light lunch or dinner.

Mango Lime Chicken Tacos Recipe

Ingredients:

For the Mango Lime Chicken:

- 1 pound boneless, skinless chicken breasts or thighs, thinly sliced
- 1 ripe mango, peeled and diced
- Juice of 2 limes
- Zest of 1 lime
- 2 tablespoons olive oil
- 2 cloves garlic, minced
- 1 teaspoon ground cumin
- 1 teaspoon chili powder
- Salt and pepper to taste

For the Mango Lime Salsa:

- 1 ripe mango, peeled and diced
- 1/2 red onion, finely chopped
- 1/4 cup fresh cilantro, chopped
- Juice of 1 lime
- Salt and pepper to taste

For Serving:

- Corn or flour tortillas
- Shredded lettuce or cabbage
- Avocado slices
- Sour cream or Greek yogurt (optional)
- Fresh lime wedges

Instructions:

1. Marinate the Chicken:

- In a bowl, combine the sliced chicken with diced mango, lime juice, lime zest, olive oil, minced garlic, ground cumin, chili powder, salt, and pepper. Toss to coat the chicken evenly. Allow it to marinate for at least 30 minutes, or refrigerate for a few hours for more flavor.

2. Cook the Chicken:

- Heat a skillet over medium-high heat. Add the marinated chicken and cook until it's cooked through and slightly caramelized, about 5-7 minutes.

3. Prepare the Mango Lime Salsa:

- In a separate bowl, combine diced mango, finely chopped red onion, chopped cilantro, lime juice, salt, and pepper to create the mango lime salsa. Mix well.

4. Warm the Tortillas:

- Warm the tortillas according to package instructions or heat them on a dry skillet for about 20 seconds on each side.

5. Assemble the Tacos:

- Spoon the cooked mango lime chicken onto each tortilla. Top with shredded lettuce or cabbage, mango lime salsa, and avocado slices.

6. Optional Toppings:

- Add a dollop of sour cream or Greek yogurt if desired. Garnish with additional cilantro and serve with fresh lime wedges.

7. Serve:

- Serve the Mango Lime Chicken Tacos immediately.

8. Enjoy:

- Enjoy these flavorful and refreshing tacos with the perfect balance of sweetness from mango, tanginess from lime, and savory grilled chicken!

These Mango Lime Chicken Tacos are a delicious fusion of sweet and savory flavors, making them a perfect choice for a quick and satisfying meal. The mango lime salsa adds a burst of freshness that complements the seasoned chicken beautifully.

Orange Cranberry Quinoa Salad Recipe

Ingredients:

For the Salad:

- 1 cup quinoa, rinsed and cooked according to package instructions
- 1 cup dried cranberries
- 1/2 cup chopped pecans or walnuts
- 1/2 cup crumbled feta cheese
- 1/4 cup red onion, finely chopped
- 2 green onions, thinly sliced
- 1 orange, peeled and segmented
- Fresh parsley for garnish

For the Orange Vinaigrette:

- Juice of 2 oranges
- 3 tablespoons olive oil
- 1 tablespoon honey
- 1 teaspoon Dijon mustard
- Salt and pepper to taste

Instructions:

1. Cook Quinoa:

- Rinse the quinoa under cold water and cook it according to package instructions. Allow it to cool to room temperature.

2. Prepare Orange Vinaigrette:

- In a small bowl, whisk together the orange juice, olive oil, honey, Dijon mustard, salt, and pepper to create the orange vinaigrette. Set aside.

3. Assemble the Salad:

- In a large salad bowl, combine the cooked quinoa, dried cranberries, chopped nuts, crumbled feta cheese, red onion, green onions, and orange segments.

4. Toss with Vinaigrette:

- Pour the prepared orange vinaigrette over the salad and toss gently to combine. Ensure that the dressing coats the ingredients evenly.

5. Garnish:

- Garnish the salad with fresh parsley for a burst of color and flavor.

6. Chill (Optional):

- Refrigerate the salad for at least 30 minutes to allow the flavors to meld, or serve it immediately.

7. Serve:

- Serve the Orange Cranberry Quinoa Salad as a refreshing and nutritious side dish or a light meal.

8. Enjoy:

- Enjoy the delightful combination of quinoa, sweet cranberries, crunchy nuts, and the citrusy goodness of oranges in this vibrant and tasty salad!

This Orange Cranberry Quinoa Salad is not only delicious but also packed with wholesome ingredients. It's a perfect choice for a light lunch, a side dish for dinner, or a refreshing contribution to potlucks and picnics.

Strawberry Basil Bruschetta Recipe

Ingredients:

For the Strawberry Basil Topping:

- 1 cup fresh strawberries, hulled and diced
- 1/4 cup fresh basil, finely chopped
- 1 tablespoon balsamic vinegar
- 1 tablespoon honey
- 1/4 teaspoon black pepper
- Pinch of salt

For the Bruschetta Base:

- Baguette or French bread, sliced
- Olive oil for brushing
- 1 clove garlic, peeled (for rubbing on the bread)

Instructions:

1. Prepare the Strawberry Basil Topping:

- In a bowl, combine the diced strawberries, finely chopped basil, balsamic vinegar, honey, black pepper, and a pinch of salt. Gently toss the ingredients together. Let the mixture sit for about 15 minutes to allow the flavors to meld.

2. Toast the Bread:

- Preheat your oven broiler or grill. Arrange the sliced baguette on a baking sheet and brush one side with olive oil. Toast under the broiler or on the grill until the edges are golden brown. Alternatively, you can use a toaster.

3. Rub with Garlic:

- While the bread is still warm, rub the toasted side with the peeled clove of garlic. This adds a subtle garlic flavor to the bruschetta.

4. Top with Strawberry Basil Mixture:

- Spoon the strawberry basil mixture generously onto the toasted side of each bread slice.

5. Serve:

- Arrange the Strawberry Basil Bruschetta on a serving platter.

6. Optional Garnish:

- Optionally, you can drizzle a little extra honey over the top for added sweetness.

7. Enjoy:

- Serve the Strawberry Basil Bruschetta immediately and savor the delightful combination of sweet strawberries, aromatic basil, and tangy balsamic vinegar!

This Strawberry Basil Bruschetta is a perfect appetizer for spring and summer gatherings. The sweet and savory combination creates a burst of freshness with every bite. It's a quick and elegant dish that's sure to impress your guests.

Peach Basil Sangria Recipe

Ingredients:

For the Sangria:

- 1 bottle of white wine (750 ml), chilled (e.g., Sauvignon Blanc or Pinot Grigio)
- 1/2 cup peach schnapps
- 1/4 cup brandy
- 1/4 cup simple syrup (adjust to taste)
- 2 ripe peaches, sliced
- 1 orange, thinly sliced
- 1 lemon, thinly sliced
- 1/4 cup fresh basil leaves, torn
- 2 cups club soda or sparkling water, chilled
- Ice cubes

For Simple Syrup:

- 1/2 cup water
- 1/2 cup granulated sugar

Instructions:

1. Make Simple Syrup (if not using store-bought):

- In a small saucepan, combine water and sugar. Heat over medium heat, stirring occasionally, until the sugar has completely dissolved. Allow the simple syrup to cool before using.

2. Prepare Fruits and Basil:

- Wash and slice the peaches, orange, and lemon. Tear the fresh basil leaves.

3. Mix Sangria:

- In a large pitcher, combine the chilled white wine, peach schnapps, brandy, and simple syrup. Stir well to mix the ingredients.

4. Add Fruits and Basil:

- Add the sliced peaches, orange slices, lemon slices, and torn basil leaves to the pitcher. Stir gently to incorporate the fruits and basil into the sangria.

5. Chill:

- Refrigerate the sangria for at least 2-4 hours, allowing the flavors to meld and the fruits to infuse the liquid.

6. Finish with Club Soda:

- Just before serving, add the chilled club soda or sparkling water to the sangria. Stir gently.

7. Serve:

- Fill glasses with ice cubes and pour the Peach Basil Sangria over the ice.

8. Garnish (Optional):

- Garnish each glass with a sprig of fresh basil or a slice of peach if desired.

9. Enjoy:

- Sip and enjoy this refreshing and fruity Peach Basil Sangria, perfect for warm weather gatherings and outdoor occasions!

This Peach Basil Sangria is a delightful twist on the classic sangria, featuring the sweet and juicy flavors of ripe peaches and the aromatic touch of fresh basil. It's a perfect drink to share with friends and family during sunny days or festive celebrations.

Caramel Apple Crisp Recipe

Ingredients:

For the Apple Filling:

- 6 cups peeled and sliced apples (e.g., Granny Smith or Honeycrisp)
- 1/4 cup granulated sugar
- 1/4 cup brown sugar, packed
- 1 tablespoon all-purpose flour
- 1 teaspoon ground cinnamon
- 1/4 teaspoon ground nutmeg
- 1/4 teaspoon salt
- 1 tablespoon lemon juice

For the Crumble Topping:

- 1 cup old-fashioned rolled oats
- 1/2 cup all-purpose flour
- 1/2 cup brown sugar, packed
- 1/4 cup chopped walnuts or pecans (optional)
- 1/2 teaspoon ground cinnamon
- 1/4 teaspoon salt
- 1/2 cup unsalted butter, cold and cubed

For Drizzling (Optional):

- Caramel sauce for serving

Instructions:

1. Preheat the Oven:

- Preheat your oven to 350°F (175°C). Grease a 9x13-inch baking dish or a similar-sized baking pan.

2. Prepare the Apple Filling:

- In a large bowl, combine the sliced apples, granulated sugar, brown sugar, flour, cinnamon, nutmeg, salt, and lemon juice. Toss until the apples are evenly coated with the mixture.

3. Transfer to Baking Dish:

    - Transfer the apple mixture to the greased baking dish, spreading it evenly.

4. Make the Crumble Topping:

    - In a separate bowl, combine rolled oats, flour, brown sugar, chopped nuts (if using), cinnamon, and salt. Add the cold, cubed butter. Using a pastry cutter or your fingers, work the butter into the dry ingredients until you have a crumbly texture.

5. Add Topping to Apples:

    - Sprinkle the crumble topping evenly over the apples in the baking dish.

6. Bake:

    - Bake in the preheated oven for 40-45 minutes or until the topping is golden brown, and the apples are tender and bubbly.

7. Cool Slightly:

    - Allow the caramel apple crisp to cool for about 10-15 minutes before serving.

8. Drizzle with Caramel (Optional):

    - If desired, drizzle caramel sauce over the top of the apple crisp before serving.

9. Serve Warm:

    - Serve the Caramel Apple Crisp warm, either on its own or with a scoop of vanilla ice cream for an extra treat.

10. Enjoy:

- Enjoy this comforting and indulgent dessert that captures the flavors of fall in every delicious bite!

Honeydew Mint Cooler Recipe

Ingredients:

- 4 cups honeydew melon, peeled, seeded, and cubed
- 1/4 cup fresh mint leaves, plus extra for garnish
- 2 tablespoons honey (adjust to taste)
- Juice of 2 limes
- 2 cups ice cubes
- 1 cup cold water
- Sparkling water (optional, for added fizz)
- Lime slices for garnish (optional)

Instructions:

1. Prepare the Honeydew:

- Peel, seed, and cube the honeydew melon to make approximately 4 cups.

2. Blend Honeydew and Mint:

- In a blender, combine the honeydew cubes, fresh mint leaves, honey, and lime juice. Blend until smooth.

3. Add Ice and Water:

- Add the ice cubes and cold water to the blender. Blend again until the mixture is well combined and has a slushy consistency.

4. Adjust Sweetness:

- Taste the cooler and adjust the sweetness by adding more honey if needed. Blend again to incorporate.

5. Strain (Optional):

- If you prefer a smoother consistency, you can strain the mixture using a fine mesh sieve to remove any pulp. This step is optional.

6. Serve:

- Pour the honeydew mint mixture into glasses.

7. Add Sparkling Water (Optional):

- For a fizzy version, top off the glasses with sparkling water. Gently stir to combine.

8. Garnish:

- Garnish each glass with fresh mint leaves and lime slices if desired.

9. Chill (Optional):

- If the ingredients were not already chilled, you can refrigerate the cooler for a short time before serving to enhance its refreshing quality.

10. Enjoy:

- Serve the Honeydew Mint Cooler immediately and enjoy this hydrating and revitalizing beverage, perfect for warm days!

This Honeydew Mint Cooler is a delightful and refreshing drink, combining the natural sweetness of honeydew with the invigorating flavor of fresh mint. It's a great way to stay cool and hydrated, especially during hot weather.

Coconut Lime Cupcakes Recipe

Ingredients:

For the Cupcakes:

- 1 and 1/2 cups all-purpose flour
- 1 and 1/2 teaspoons baking powder
- 1/4 teaspoon salt
- 1/2 cup unsalted butter, softened
- 1 cup granulated sugar
- 2 large eggs
- 1 teaspoon vanilla extract
- 1/2 cup coconut milk
- Zest of 2 limes
- 2 tablespoons fresh lime juice

For the Coconut Lime Frosting:

- 1/2 cup unsalted butter, softened
- 2 cups powdered sugar
- 1/4 cup coconut milk
- 1 teaspoon coconut extract (optional)
- Zest of 1 lime
- Shredded coconut for garnish (optional)
- Lime slices for garnish (optional)

Instructions:

For the Cupcakes:

1. Preheat the Oven:

- Preheat your oven to 350°F (175°C). Line a cupcake tin with paper liners.

2. Prepare Dry Ingredients:

- In a bowl, whisk together the flour, baking powder, and salt. Set aside.

3. Cream Butter and Sugar:

- In a large mixing bowl, cream together the softened butter and granulated sugar until light and fluffy.

4. Add Eggs and Vanilla:

- Add the eggs one at a time, beating well after each addition. Mix in the vanilla extract.

5. Incorporate Dry Ingredients:

- Gradually add the dry ingredients to the wet ingredients, alternating with the coconut milk. Begin and end with the dry ingredients. Mix until just combined.

6. Add Lime Zest and Juice:

- Stir in the lime zest and fresh lime juice until evenly distributed in the batter.

7. Fill Cupcake Liners:

- Divide the batter evenly among the cupcake liners, filling each about two-thirds full.

8. Bake:

- Bake in the preheated oven for 18-20 minutes or until a toothpick inserted into the center of a cupcake comes out clean.

9. Cool:

- Allow the cupcakes to cool in the tin for a few minutes, then transfer them to a wire rack to cool completely.

For the Coconut Lime Frosting:

1. Beat Butter:

- In a separate bowl, beat the softened butter until creamy.

2. Add Powdered Sugar:

- Gradually add the powdered sugar to the butter, beating well after each addition.

3. Incorporate Coconut Milk and Lime Zest:

- Mix in the coconut milk and lime zest. Add coconut extract if using.

4. Beat Until Smooth:

- Continue beating until the frosting is smooth and fluffy.

Assembly:

1. Frost Cupcakes:

- Once the cupcakes are completely cooled, frost them with the Coconut Lime Frosting using a piping bag or a spatula.

2. Garnish (Optional):

- Optionally, garnish each cupcake with shredded coconut and a slice of lime.

3. Enjoy:

- Enjoy these Coconut Lime Cupcakes with a perfect balance of tropical flavors!

These Coconut Lime Cupcakes are a delightful treat with a tropical twist. The combination of coconut and lime creates a refreshing and flavorful dessert that's perfect for any occasion.

Passion Fruit Sorbet Recipe

Ingredients:

- 2 cups fresh passion fruit pulp (about 10-12 passion fruits)
- 1 cup granulated sugar
- 1 cup water
- 2 tablespoons fresh lime or lemon juice

Instructions:

1. Extract Passion Fruit Pulp:

- Cut the passion fruits in half and scoop out the pulp using a spoon. Collect about 2 cups of fresh passion fruit pulp.

2. Make Simple Syrup:

- In a saucepan, combine the granulated sugar and water. Heat over medium heat, stirring occasionally, until the sugar dissolves completely. Allow the mixture to cool to room temperature.

3. Combine Ingredients:

- In a blender, combine the passion fruit pulp, simple syrup, and fresh lime or lemon juice. Blend until smooth.

4. Strain (Optional):

- If you prefer a smoother sorbet, you can strain the mixture using a fine mesh sieve to remove seeds and any remaining pulp. This step is optional.

5. Chill Mixture:

- Place the passion fruit mixture in the refrigerator to chill for at least 2 hours or until thoroughly cold.

6. Churn in Ice Cream Maker:

- Transfer the chilled mixture to an ice cream maker and churn according to the manufacturer's instructions until it reaches a sorbet consistency.

7. Freeze:

- Transfer the churned sorbet into a lidded container and freeze for an additional 2-4 hours or until firm.

8. Serve:

- Scoop the Passion Fruit Sorbet into bowls or cones.

9. Garnish (Optional):

- Garnish with fresh mint leaves, a wedge of passion fruit, or a slice of lime for an extra touch.

10. Enjoy:

- Enjoy the refreshing and tropical flavor of homemade Passion Fruit Sorbet!

This homemade Passion Fruit Sorbet is a delightful and exotic frozen treat. The natural sweetness and tangy notes of passion fruit create a refreshing dessert that's perfect for cooling down on warm days.

www.ingramcontent.com/pod-product-compliance
Lightning Source LLC
LaVergne TN
LVHW081552060526
838201LV00054B/1875